# CLARE BOOTHE LUCE

# CLARE BOOTHE LUCE

## WILFRID SHEED

E. P. DUTTON • NEW YORK

Copyright © 1982 by Wilfrid Sheed

Published in the United States by
Dutton Publishing Inc.,
2 Park Avenue, New York, N.Y. 10016

Library of Congress Cataloging in Publication Data

Sheed, Wilfrid
    Clare Booth Luce.

    Includes bibliographical references.
    1. Luce, Clare Booth,     2. Ambassadors—
United States—Biography.   3. Legislators—United
States—Biography.   4. Dramatists, American—20th
century—Biography.   5. Journalists—United States—
Biography.   I. Title.
E748.L894S53      973.91'092'4   [B]      81-9882
                                          AACR2

ISBN: 0-525-03055-7

Published simultaneously in Canada by Clarke,
Irwin & Company Limited, Toronto and Vancouver

Designed by Nicola Mazzella

10  9  8  7  6  5  4  3  2  1

First Edition

*To the late Ann Brokaw.*

# CONTENTS

# PREFACE

"She was the best of dames, she was the worst of dames" my father suggested as an opener for this book. Just about everything I've read about Clare Boothe Luce so far has taken one view or the other, painting her as either an angel or a dragon lady, according to taste. Clearly this is getting us nowhere.

What follows is not a biography. In fact, I'm not dead sure what it is. I had thought of simply saying, as one might of a novel, that it contains everything that interests me about the subject and leaves out everything that doesn't. But this is not quite true.

Clare Luce cooperated with me, out of curiosity I imagine, and attached no conditions whatever (she hasn't seen the manuscript) except for two small ones, one of which I have cavalierly overridden: namely, that I call her "Luce" throughout, as I would call her husband Harry "Luce" if the book were about him. This proved unworkable because for one thing she wasn't always a Luce but at various times a Boothe and a Brokaw, and for another I decided I would probably call Harry "Harry" too, if I ever had to.

The second condition was that I not make this an "as told to" book. I had never intended to, out of very vanity. But I now find myself with yards of unused tape and notes, some of them very interesting indeed. Perhaps some other time. I have also received

1

yards of outside help, vignettes, insights, the works, some of it wildly conflicting, until I began to hallucinate a Picasso portrait with three noses and eyes like clarinet stops. Because of her several careers, Clare's life fairly bulges with characters, and the conclusions you reach depend very much on which hundred or so you've talked to.

So in the end, I decided to squeeze the juice out of the more plausible accounts and otherwise stick to my own version, which has at least the virtue of unity. There is definitely only one Clare Luce in this book, or at the outside two. My tone will be, by the nature of the case, informal, epistolary: I'm writing about a living person, not a monument. And although there is enough left over by the end for at least another book or two, when I saw, in these pages, a portrait I recognized, I stopped.

# CHAPTER ONE

# *The Summer* - I

The summer was 1949 and time marches on. In setting up the scenery for what follows, my mind jumps first to the rhetoric, even before it gets to the cars and hats: not that everyone in the forties talked like a "March of Time" newsreel, any more than everyone wore a Dior gown. Fashion is simply an index to how much a given generation will swallow. Hence, anyway, Henry Luce.

The thing is, he was not alone. Although his Tory news magazine may have carried the Mock Portentous style to the end of the line and beyond, so did Edward R. Murrow's broadcasts, which were a liberal's delight; after thirteen years of Roosevelt, hokum came easily, to Americans of all stripes.* From the *Reader's Digest* to Disney Studios, and taking in the one hundred great books in Chicago, a mighty web of artificiality stretched across the land in the forties, so seamless that one was barely aware of it. In this atmosphere, Bishop Fulton Sheen seemed perfectly natural, and so did Norman Vincent Peale and General MacArthur. So if Clare and Harry Luce seem a little unreal today, it should be stressed right off that most everyone else did then, too. The whole forefront of

---

* FDR's "A date which will live in infamy" could have come straight from a "March of Time" documentary. Contemporary rivals often resemble each other more than they resemble their future sympathizers.

American life had a strange gleam to it, like a starlet's smile, as wartime propaganda turned its incandescence on peace and tried to make it glow like World War II: patriotism, religion, optimism for its own sweet sake—anything to ward off depression.

When I met Clare Luce that summer, I didn't know much about her, except that she was undoubtedly one of the ten most and least—admired less than Eleanor Roosevelt, but better dressed than the Pope, a celebrity at large who lived on lists. She was also "glamorous," which was considered a bad but necessary thing in social America—like whores in a mining town. Somebody had to do it. By chance I had read her play *The Women* and made the general mistake of assuming she was one of the characters in that grammar of bitchery. But since it didn't sound much worse than life in a boarding school, I didn't hold it against her.

Outside of that, the big news at our place was that she had become a Catholic, which wiped everything clean; short of Hitler, but probably not Göring, any conversion was a cause for uncomplicated rejoicing. My family was fundamentally apolitical anyway; the business of life was finding God, the rest was negotiable. So Stalin or Mao Tse-tung would have been equally acceptable, if they could have cleared the technicalities.

The branch of the Church Clare had entered was considered something of a cultural outback (the United States was listed as missionary territory as late as the twenties). So one fancies a hasty attempt to straighten up the parlor and invite the most presentable Hottentots over to meet our fancy new member. This had to include my parents, Frank Sheed and Maisie Ward, who ran a publishing house (arrestingly named Sheed & Ward), which in those days cross-pollinated European and American writers so effectively that something called "the Catholic Revival" was in the works. In fact, this revival was probably responsible for converts like Clare in the first place.

Anyhow, we were all checked in early: my Australian father, whom I'll introduce at the proper time, and my very English mother, who, I think, never quite saw the *point* of Clare, though she had no special objection (my mother never saw the point of the Japanese either). Both of them met Clare and a fellow convert called Greta Palmer, and reported that the two were like Roman matrons in the first century who'd just Christianized and were on fire with excitement.

My sister met the Luces before I did and came back glowing over *Harry*, whom she found quick and witty—an impression which has since been confirmed by absolutely nobody, but which tells something of his response to young, good-looking women. (A side result of that dinner was that Rosemary began to get some of Clare's cast-off dresses, which the latter ran through at some two a day—yet Rosemary wasn't even voted best-dressed on the block.)

Nobody can remember now why I was invited, sight unseen, to the Luce house in Ridgefield, Connecticut—it seemed like a colossal absence of mind on somebody's part. Anyhow, the best way to get there was to bum a ride with Harry, who was chauffeured up and back on weekends. I seem to remember his sitting as far away from me as you can get in a large limousine, and either reading or staring out the window the whole way, neither fast nor witty. My feeling was that he was as scared of me as I was of him, which would have left him pretty close to jelly. But I have since observed that lots of editors (Harold Ross, William Shawn, my old friend Harold Hayes of *Esquire*) are occupationally shy, because almost every conversation includes a potential imposition.

In Luce's case, I suspect he summed me up with brutal accuracy as someone he didn't have much to learn from, certainly not enough to crank up his famous stammer for; and indeed the only times he was ever to speak easily to me were times when he sensed a possible area of expertise. Since he didn't expect an eighteen-year-old to know anything at all, he was always slightly incredulous when he came upon these. "How do *you* know about David Belasco? He died before you were born," he would bristle. "There are books, written records," I muttered. "Whut, whut?" His deafness was such that I was not sure he ever heard anything I said, so I was off balance when he did catch something like Belasco. His wonderment over that may have said something about his magazines: he believed that names make news, but that the public didn't know more than about twelve of them.

Anyway, bristle is what he did—with those eyebrows it was hard not to—and after a stretch in his silent company, Clare came as a sun-shower of relief. Her face was as clear as Harry's was clouded, with a radiance that was not simply sexy, as advertised, but—the word right then was simply "cheerful," like lights going on in a dark house. It was almost as if she had chosen Luce as a foil, to emphasize her own good qualities, which included manifest ease, friendliness, and uptake: you didn't have to tell her you were tired or hungry or, as you might with Harry, that you'd just fainted.

She met me at the door of what I can only call their Chinese southern plantation, and her cool voice might have been designed for welcoming nervous people. She spoke slower than she had to, in a slightly facetious drawl that picked up stray bits of humor as it went along, and in later years she could slow this down even more, to the very brink of woolliness. But you could tell this was a stage effect; her mind could always speed up, depending on the speed of the game, and I have seldom seen anyone hit a wisecrack past her.

Under the public carapace one expected something a great deal harder than the Clare that greeted me, and I was somewhat stupefied by her gentleness as she showed me around what was to be my room for the weekend. "The bathroom explains itself," she said. It came as a further shock, so strangely were they floodlit in those days, that power people could still be reasonably natural around the house, even if Harry's cadence sounded like Walter Winchell calling all the ships at sea.

By dinnertime I had met their set: the Pope, Nehru, guys like that. It was jarring at first (Winston who? I knew a guy called Chiang myself) but undeniably exhilarating. Although the mundane small talk was taken care of by the servants—so that if we talked about, say, crabgrass it was always the National Problem of crabgrass—the small change about Madame Chiang or Winnie was neighborly and irreverent. The Luces' hero worship didn't cramp their style, it only dictated the subject matter. Churchill *was* their neighbor; I never met the people next door, if there were any. Clare, with her amused voice, reduced the Great World to room-size instead.

So I was surprised later that summer to hear Clare's voice on the radio: it was pitched high and quite artificial, as if in the early days of microphones. She was paying a tribute to Eleanor Roosevelt, but for a moment I thought she was imitating her instead. The Clare I met had no connection with this. She seemed soft and almost spectral, like an apparition, or a very understanding nun. Quiet, translucent, a very light presence. If she really was a bitch, she was playing a deep game.

My weekend room turned gradually into my summer room, until I was moved to even grander quarters. I felt no burning inclination to leave a house where you could whistle for breakfast whenever you liked and have it served up with four newspapers, and she showed no overt inclination to get rid of me. Harry seemed faintly surprised to see me weekend after weekend, and mildly bored, but all in all quite gentlemanly about it. It seems he only appeared to bristle: underneath, he was, in equal parts, kind and indifferent.

But that first tour of the guest room did not quite separate me from Clare the public woman. Because on every sheet and towel and every matchbox—in fact on anything that could bear initials—there were hers, emblazoned. Vanity, of course, but like all her vices so candid and exuberant as to leave one slightly stunned. As retold, it may sound like the Bad Queen surrounded by her own reflection. But in the flesh, it was more like someone who's just come into money and hasn't gotten over it yet. This is an *American* story.

At the time, she was in the process of recovering from Politics, but it didn't show. In fact, her breezy serenity suggested that she had never had a bad day in her life—an infuriating quality in an enemy, and one that I take it she'd worked on. She did insist she would not run for office again, but not for reasons of trauma. She said the trouble with politics was that you could never admit a mistake, which hardly suited her confessional mood of the moment. But she had a yet more solid and unnegotiable reason than that. She was determined that her Catholic conversion not seem like a political trick. Connecticut was a good Catholic constituency, and she was particularly popular with the Italian hat makers of Danbury, as I recall. Rich converts were a joke of the period anyway; but a political one had no hope at all of being taken seriously. In fact, Clare told a joke that summer about Tom Clark, who allegedly wanted the Catholic seat on the Supreme Court and had asked someone how long it took to qualify. So it was on her mind.

Instead she tried, with her usual cyclonic determination, to become a private person with an inner life, and that's what I walked in on the middle of. It was a good year for Republicans to go private anyway; Harry Truman, whom Harry Luce considered the *reductio ad absurdum* of the common man, had just pulled off his miracle, so Washington was closed, as were the foreign embassies. And Clare had done everything else. Privacy looked for a wild moment like a promising adventure.

It wasn't to last, of course, even as long as Thomas Merton's silence; but it was real while it lasted—not, to cite her favorite comic character, a Garbo-like affectation. We talked about it too much for that. She was, I understood, determinedly trying to simplify herself, to recapture the things a precocious person misses, like a math prodigy learning baseball. In her case, this included a child's sense of religious wonder, which is a frustrating quarry for a sophisticate. But she enjoyed simplicity and found, as with everything else, that she was not altogether bad at it.

One of her models was St. Thérèse of Lisieux, otherwise known as the Little Flower and virtually the patron of anti-celebrity. Thérèse, Clare told me, had also made a deliberate choice to be unspectacular: to sanctify the small things in life and let the big ones go. Clare was fascinated by how one did this: day upon day without highlights or payoffs. She saw that it was the right thing to do. "Pinprick martyrdom" she called it, in an essay she wrote about the Saints in 1952, and she described Thérèse's "little way of the Cross" as the heaviest cross there is: the cross of getting through the day anonymously and perfectly. When I talked to her recently about this, she told me that curiosity had finally goaded her into trying the "little way" for twenty-four hours, at the end of which she realized that sanctity was not for her. "Too strenuous," said the retired dynamo.

I have long since wondered why I wasn't thrown out of this not notoriously patient woman's house. Perhaps it was her own gesture toward pinprick martyrdom. I was part of St. Thérèse's "little way." Another reason might be that her daughter's death was still a running wound, and she may have enjoyed having something like a son around the place. Her marriage had obviously cooled, although she always liked *talking* to Harry, a taste I could never fathom. ("He was never *boring.*") She told me good-naturedly that I looked like a bright sort of chap who might have an idea every now and then— which was indeed my schedule. And thus I also satisfied a deep passion in her, which was simply to instruct.

And instruct she did all golden summer long, starting with a diet lunch (she's a late sleeper, or at least a late surfacer) and shunting in fits and starts through the day, and often winding up around one in the morning in her room or mine. If the reader is wondering if there was any *Tea and Sympathy* about this, I can only pass on my hazy impression that she was too courteous to rule out the possibility. One evening, she reclined on my bed in a way which was over too fast to be called an invitation by anyone short of Harpo Marx, but which suggested the possibility: in a different time and circumstance, perhaps.

It was an innocent period, especially for young Catholics, and the idea of an eighteen-year-old boy making time with a forty-six-year-old woman did not come naturally, or at all. But Clare was like a southern belle, for whom a certain flirtatiousness is simple good manners, and she did not, to my surprise, necessarily turn it up for important people whom she preferred to impress as an equal, but for people she didn't need to impress. On the other side of this lay a black mood, also private—a cold, inexplicable burst of silence, of which I experienced just one, which lasted two days and disappeared as strangely as it came. I had done some small thing to provoke her, but for the life of me cannot remember what it was, except for its sheer smallness: on the order of declining to drive with her to the village or go to the movies.

Unlike her image, she was the opposite of glacial, and unlike such later feminists as Gloria Steinem, she didn't seem easily able to suspend sexual differences to make an argument, but almost had to change personalities to do so, turning from my sunny friend of daylight to a species of schoolmarm at table. No doubt a serious woman had to be very no-nonsense indeed (or else very plain-looking) to get a fair hearing in those days. When Clare's sex appeal was turned off, it was like a new ice age. Or so I remember it. In this chapter, I am still trying to be eighteen and see only what I saw then; and what I saw was a "drenchingly beautiful" (as Cecil Beaton allegedly called her), slightly coquettish woman—in the sense that one might say lightly perfumed, not *dead* sure it's there at all—who could douse it completely in front of an audience. And with Clare, three could be an audience.

Depending on who they were. That summer, a steady trickle of stuffed shirts (a phrase she claims with good reason to have coined herself) seemed to pass through, and for them she would on occasion pontificate quite sexlessly, halfway into her public manner. Her ardent desire to be taken seriously could have made her unintentionally funny, except for a strange note of self-mockery, which suggested it was meant to be funny.

What I could not understand at the time was why, with a world of company to choose from, the Luces settled for this particular gang. To put it delicately, they were the dullest people I had ever met. I was too inexperienced to make fine distinctions between politicos and businessmen—in fact, in a sheltered life I had never met a businessman, only publishers—so now I merely see a collage of large, slow-thinking men of the kind one deduced from old *Time* cover stories, and I remember conjecturing that perhaps Clare preferred slightly dumb company in order to shine the more—a neat theory, because it also helped to explain Harry.

But it didn't explain the brilliant friends she'd had in the past. So I also wondered briefly if she had put clever people behind her, as part of her sinful youth. Now I think she was simply taking what the casting director sent her way. As an actor-politician, you check the house each night and soldier on. These, I suppose, were Harry's power people, the world of *Fortune*, not *Variety*, or even Drew Pearson, and perhaps she liked to impress them as Harry's consort, and possibly even Superior, at his own game, as panjandrum and chairman of the board. She is a games player above all.

Anyway, two senior executives was a crowd to be addressed, but two friends was blessedly not. When her old chum George Waldo of the Hartford *Courant* came round, or her schoolmate Buffy Cobb, she was as girlish and funny as she was one-on-one. Waldo claimed to have an electric blanket that ejected him gently when he was warm on both sides. His passion was reforestation, and I think of him whenever I fly over Connecticut. Buffy was like the heroine's pal in a movie: raspy, funny, and so ugly she was attractive. Clare made no attempt at all to impress these far more intelligent but less important people; nor—and this should have told me something—did she try very hard with such old-shoe politicians as Speaker of the House Joe Martin or Senator Brewster, whom she seemed to treat as a lovable tradesman, as opposed to Harry's lords of the earth. I got a glimmer one evening when somebody asked Martin what he thought of the upcoming Belgian election, and his answer suggested that he hadn't known for sure that Belgium had elections. After four years in such company, businessmen *might* come to seem more important.

The notable thing was that in all the reams of anecdote and instruction that I received from her that summer, there was never a trace of the dining room autocrat. Even the same clever-clever theories ("armies from two degrees of latitude north always win") sounded quite different in private: whimsical, ingenious, what the English call try-ons. The striking thing about them was their fecundity. Good, or bad, she sprayed you with a fresh set every night. But delivered even a little more solemnly for some paltry vice-president of Pan Am, they sounded as if she'd been preparing them all week. Her spontaneity, which was genuine, always had a curious, rehearsed quality, as if she'd tested it in her head at top speed, before reciting it to some favorite English teacher of long ago. Anyway, I decided then and there that she was gallantly trying to adjust herself, as a good wife should.

I did not, as a tongue-tied Oscar Wilde, understand the deeper nature of her challenge: which was, how *was* a woman supposed to be clever over brandy and cigars? In her youth, one simply left the room or was pushed. Now one stayed—but then what? Was Clare supposed to bring feminine lightness and caprice from the next room? Or was she, like Burlington Bertie dressed up in tails, expected to act like a man, laying down the law and topping the other fellow? Being Clare, she of course tried both—which was plucky or overweening, or both. She was, after all, a U.S. congresswoman, and also a Broadway wit, a salon keeper and a salon star, for which combination there were no instructions, and precious few precedents. It was a brand-new territory, outside the tiny compound where women lived in those days. Clare was a pioneer not just during office hours but every breathing minute: a role that might have taxed St. Thérèse herself.

Out of all the conversation that lashes one during a lifetime, why does one remember this and not that? Because of the precision with which it hits the nervous system, I suppose. "Watch out for envy," she said once, apropos of nothing. We were doing a jigsaw, which means talking but absolutely no thinking, a dream state. "I don't see why anyone would envy a guy with polio," I said, as I pored over the pale greens. She said, "Yes, I guess that might slow them down some. But they'll find a way."

Another time she asked me if I'd ever had a photograph taken that I really liked. I admitted a certain warmth toward my latest passport photo, which was indeed stunning. "Does it make you look like a gangster or a poet?" she asked. "Gangster," I preened—only realizing months later that this was the perfect question to ask a teen-ager, to prink up his pride without actually flattering him. She was marvelous at this: building one's confidence by indirection. "Gangster" was of course the right answer, and she smiled maternal confirmation.

She talked a lot that summer about the things she'd done just to prove a woman could do them, or at least combine them; her study was hung like a star's dressing room with pictures of herself in her roles, and in so many of them there was no other woman in sight. Everywhere she went, she was the first, or one of the first. The dilemma of the dinner table was duplicated many times over: how does a glamour puss deliver a keynote speech? Make them forget, against their senses, that she's a woman? Or be a *heavyweight* glamour puss? My first view of Clare's career was as a series of tactical problems: only later did I hear words like "triumphant" and "disgraceful" applied to the solutions.

For every problem Clare faced, she created another for those around her. Because her straight men were just as much at sea in Clare's scenario as she was. I surmised both from observation and from hearing her anecdotes that men dealt with her awkwardly and had to be dealt with right back, according to their kind. Some were irredeemably competitive and had to be trounced. Some were wolfishly smitten by her, and these must be lectured to, with the granny glasses down; but others *she* was smitten by right back, and this was more complicated—sometimes much more complicated. But that summer she was not being smitten by anybody.

Although I have since learned that her marriage to Harry was cooler even than it looked (his apparent indifference was aimed not at me but at the weekend in general), Clare gave no hint of outside love interests. One evening she exceeded her one old-fashioned limit and got a touch giggly with a handsome dinner escort, and I thought something might be in the wind. But I never saw the chap again. And George Waldo was strictly a court jester in our little play.

Since the house was strewn with Burns Mantle's best plays of this year and George Jean Nathan's best plays of that and more pictures of actors on stages than I hope to see again, it is small wonder that I still picture Ridgefield as a stage setting: visitors entering Right the large, slightly oriental living room, talking lightly or seriously as the author decides, depending on mood and the cast's limitations, and exiting Left onto the patio. Gruff, typecast publisher absentmindedly takes wrong arm of mystery blonde, who smiles secretly. In the background, Ezio Pinza bawls "Some Enchanted Evening" over and over, on the first LP I have heard yet, and Alfred Drake opens in Venice with Cole Porter: all very Broadway.

It wasn't just Burns Mantle, it was a retired playwright still doing what she did best. Clare's direction was firm but unobtrusive. We appeared to drift, but it was *always* her play. The best of her dialogue was serious light comedy, as if Neil Simon had undertaken to write the life of Arnold Toynbee. If on rare occasions the guests were up to it, one got a genuine sense of journalistic aristocracy—a contradiction that Harry dedicated his life to. It was also, to round out the fantasy, the best second act Clare could come up with for herself, and I was playing the moonfaced youth from the provinces who would years from now try to write it all down.

# CHAPTER TWO

# *The Summer* - II

If it rained that summer, I don't remember it. All I see is a succession of P. G. Wodehouse days rolling out, for which I would pay dearly when I got back to real life: mornings spent reading between the dapples on the patio; afternoons, watching Dodger games on the outsize TV—still a juicy novelty; then a dip in the pool with my hostess, who had once had an Olympic tryout. She raced me one time, and I beat her by inches, and it took me twenty years to figure out that she'd thrown the race.

Dinner had a tendency to be the same, too. Icy shrimp salad, steak—Harry never saw the need for anything else, and Clare's own food tastes are still pretty narrow: stage food to go with the dialogue. Also, she seems to think she has a weight problem around the thighs, and perhaps she has: it's one of those metaphysical distinctions only thin women can see. When Harry was around, I had to wear a necktie (no jacket) at table, and he gave me a blue one with some of the hundred great books etched on it, which I wore all summer. Just a lick of the ceremonial was enough. Harry was not as starchy as he looked (it would have been difficult), nor as puritanical. "He wasn't stuffy," says Clare, adding, "He may have been constipated." He liked *his* second old-fashioned before dinner, even though it invariably meant postponing a meal that he always insisted be served on time. Clare finally worked out a scam with the cook whereby "on time" always meant twenty minutes late—which was typical of a childlike, almost kittenish fondness she had for her late-Victorian husband. It is perhaps no coincidence that she was one of the original backers of *Life with Father*.

Over dinner, Harry would bark out his latest excitements like a kid in a show-and-tell class. He had always just discovered some red-hot theologian or a new theory about the American Proposition (which Clare christened the Amprop). Or tonight he might be shocked by the sales of tranquilizers since the war and the peptic ulcer boom, indicating that all was not well with the American soul; or he might be dazzled by the number of trucks end to end it would take to deliver *Life* magazine every week. Then there was an article, I believe by Rachel Carson herself, which gave a foretaste of her own *Silent Spring*. Might the Luces themselves be guilty of using pesticides? What goes in that garden anyway? Must look into it.

Harry's conversation was like a magazine layout. One weekend he announced, "I put *Life* to bed this week. Feels good to be an editor again." Otherwise he affected semi-retirement, suggesting that his magazines edited themselves by now, a half-truth that fooled me for years.

Later we would adjourn to the jigsaw puzzle, where after Harry had intoned a blessing—"Man is a puzzle-solving animal" or some such great thought—we would fall to muttering and gibbering as puzzle solvers will. The puzzles themselves were eye-popping: especially designed for Clare at, I believe, one hundred dollars a shot, 1949 money; they were so finely cut out of such good wood that you could hang them on the wall afterwards—and so pretty that it would have been a pleasure. And one of the pieces was always in the shape of Clare's logo, the omnipresent *CBL*.

Naturally, they came in plain boxes so we never knew what we were getting at. Hence we'd each pounce on a color and worry it around, with Clare staring regally down through her lorgnette and Harry darting glances left and right to see how the others were doing. "That's some puzzling," he grunted, after I'd erected a gray warehouse with lettering on it (didn't he know that was easy?), but generally Clare was fastest and Harry a close second. Their concentration was immense and I reckon we polished off a couple of these monsters a week, including a Matisse that defied description even when complete. (Incidentally, I exaggerate Luce's style when I have him constantly grunting and barking, but he did sound funny.) Clare once made me shut my eyes when the puzzle was done and asked me to describe the details: a test of observation, so she said. Play and self-improvement were the same impulse with her, and I never know even now when she will come up with, say, some underwater exercise that may or may not give you a whole new neck; trying it is the fun.

My reading, which tapered off the waking day, on nights when Clare was trying to write or plan her life, included Krafft-Ebing for laughs (sexologists are the funniest writers around) and bound volumes of *Vanity Fair* for instruction. This latter struck me then as the best magazine I had ever seen, not excluding *The New Yorker:* it was packed not only with humorists, who all seem good when you're eighteen, but the best portrait photographers in the business and some pretty good color and line drawing too. But best of all it was suffused with the aura of my current favorite subject, the twenties sophisticates, whom I pictured, for some strange reason, as jolly good fellows.

The bound volumes covered all of Clare's five years there, for two of which she was editor in chief, so I peppered her with questions about these titans. "The Algonquin crowd was too much for me," she said surprisingly; "I couldn't compete with them." She singled out George Kaufman as a particular tiger, and she mentioned a nightmarish bridge game with the Marx Brothers, with Harpo blowing out his bubble gum a little bit further each time she bid, until she burst into tears.

Since Clare was a pretty fair bridge player, it seems likely the Algonquin gang was out to get her even more than they were out to get most people. There seemed to be that inevitable feeling that she had bought her way in with her looks, that she didn't belong, which has followed her everywhere and shaped her view of life from Newport to Harpo. Anyway, after a couple of sessions, she was not invited back by that coven of killers.

Kaufman, a man who could charm people with coldness (like JFK), epitomizes her relationship with Broadway. The Great Collaborator, who wrote hits with everyone under the sun, but couldn't or wouldn't write them by himself, actually play doctored *The Women* for Clare after the Round Table broke up. And she was still terrified of him.

I don't know whether there was something artificial about her manner then that suggested that she was cheating even when she wasn't, or whether it was the Aryan Princess in her, the Wasp misfit. Because from the evidence of the bound volumes, she had every right to be editor of *Vanity Fair* and she did a very professional job of it. But this snub from the sophisticates may have influenced her later choice of companions and indirectly of politics. At least there was no chance of one of Harry's baby tycoons blowing his gum at her or shooting her down verbally.

But her feelings about what is vaguely called Broadway did not on the whole strike me as hostile or anxious. She liked Robert Benchley (although she claimed that she had never heard him say anything funny, and even that she and Frank Crowninshield had invented some of his attributed wisecracks: unbelievable, but that's what she said) and Heywood Broun. She liked Oscar Levant up to a point, as a shy, surly, excruciatingly (even his delivery suggested a difficult stool) witty youth, who couldn't believe it if you were nice to him, but would then be very sweet in return. She thought George Gershwin one of the most modest and delightful men she had ever met—a subtle judgment, because superficially he must have been one of the vainest. She felt that George couldn't get over being around all these important people, and that his famous rush for the piano was partly caused by this: the piano was his justification for being there. (It may say something about songwriters in general that she considered Irving Berlin the truly vainest man she ever met—praise from a master, he might retort. Irving, she said, fairly reeked vanity.)

Perhaps most surprisingly, she had contracted a lifelong friendship with Noël Coward, though she found his boyfriends rather second-rate. (Otherwise, she expressed no special feeling about homosexuals, one way or the other.) And Noël Coward later that very year was to sing a duet with my father, who is not publicly known for his singing, at Clare's house in Hollywood. The song was Berlin's "Ragtime Violin," c. 1911, and may or may not have ended with a buck and wing.

Talking of Hollywood, Clare told me that actors go to bed thinking they're Gary Cooper, with partners who believe them, so that breakfast in Bel Air is simply awful: breakfast is bad anywhere, of course, but suppose you actually *are* Gary Cooper? or Clare Luce? And have to live up to it over the toast? She spoke of her friend Loretta Young's taking two hours to primp before dinner for one; and showed me with glee how the likes of Miss Young taped their loose skin under their hair (Clare obviously had no need of such ruses).

My hunch was that, if anything, Clare missed those people, knives and all. She was especially careful not to say anything nasty about Dorothy Parker, supposedly her insult-archrival, or Dorothy Thompson, her political one (famous women were commonly paired off like this): but then she seldom spoke ill of other women, unless you include the inevitable imitation of Eleanor Roosevelt (good) and some grisly accounts of Wallis Simpson in wartime, clearly rooting for a Nazi victory. "A whole nation against one lone woman" was how the Duchess described her relationship with embattled Britain in 1940: which Clare, who has been accused of grandiosity herself, found sickeningly funny. Otherwise, if she had been catty once upon a time, there was practically no trace of it now.

This was her Summer to be good, and I would guess she worked very hard at it. For some reason, being good seemed to consist above all of keeping out of public life, which would not be that hard for most of us but was a full-time job for her. One could judge the force of ambition that had got her this far from the giant grappling she was engaged in to tame it now. Martin and Brewster roguishly talked about a Senate seat, and she seemed amused by this and did not slam the door, but she limited her own king-making talk to other people. She may have been flattered, but not flattered enough to go clawing and scratching again for the crown.

In fact, there was no specific attraction in the public arena: it was just the arena itself. She noted wryly that she'd been dropped from the Ten Best-Dressed list since her conversion, and I suppose that sort of thing must hurt a little. (To get on the list, she explained, you simply hire the most famous designer and just sit back. And don't change your religion, presumably.) On the plus side, she was glad not to have "the best legs in Washington" anymore, partly because the competition wasn't that great (Margaret Chase Smith?), and partly because "I want to be known for my other end." (I became dimly aware even then that her "other end" was her *real* obsession in life.) But more to the point was the question of what you *do* with retirement. Hobbies, of course, always hobbies. Improving the mind. Praying. But then what?

All Summer, she tried to write something worthy, but she complained to me that she had lost her talent since becoming a Catholic—"You should have seen me in the old days"—and in a sense she had. Because her best work had always had some bite in it, and she felt that that was forbidden her now.

I wish I had told her that it wasn't necessary to be *quite* this

good, that for instance Evelyn Waugh was a Catholic,* but it was a
very fervent time in American church history. Being a Catholic was
a full-time occupation, and not an ornament to add to your list of
clubs. You couldn't just find Jesus and be on your way. Clare didn't
want a single neck-wrenching like that, but full membership in a
Universal Church, a body that could stand up to her and say yes,
you may have to sacrifice your talent if it comes to that. Your fabu-
lous drive to succeed can go too. In the eye of God, it is too small to
bother with. She *wanted* that.

The nature of this kind of conversion is important to distin-
guish from the latest crop, because it defines our subject: to a Catholic, meeting Jesus is something you do objectively, either in sacra-
mental fellowship or by helping the poor and downtrodden. Any
other use of the phrase is either meaningless or blasphemously
pretentious. God is reached through man—Jesus *is* the poor man,
the levite, the neighbor—and not directly by the likes of us. So
Clare was not in search of a private, subjective experience, which
the Church frowned on mightily in those days (it is less harsh now),
but of an objective Other that was bigger than she was, and that
could put her strivings in perspective.

At any rate, we talked a lot about the Church, and it was quite
pleasant to be the expert for a change. She assumed I wouldn't
think much of her former guru, Fulton Sheen, who could be quite
the ham in public. "Although he's really just as intelligent as you
are, whoever you are." I wasn't surprised, since Sheen was an old
friend of my father's, and I knew that his simple peasant approach
to Catholicism was carefully calibrated to his audiences. Sheen
would have stood on his head and whistled "When the Saints Go
Marching In" between his teeth to win souls, and I couldn't see
anything wrong with that at the time.

Since Sheen, she had had a hard time finding priests who were
not either wowed by her fame, or full of beatific plans for spending
her money. I assured her that she was moving in the wrong circles,
and that I had known some unworldly, intelligent priests who could
reasonably be presumed celebrity-proof. But when it came to naming one, it turned out they were all abroad. Even the guys who are
unworldly around the block stiffen next to celebrity: it's a prehis-
toric reflex. Maybe the Church could stand up to her, but its repre-

---

* A year or so later, Evelyn administered the lesson himself, summoning the wine list at
a top-dollar bistro they'd taken him to and stiffing the Luces for the largest restaurant bill (if
we except the Windsors, as we must) in their history.

sentatives couldn't. "Will you be working on a new play, Mrs. Luce? Will you be running again for Congress?" It's a fat lot of help running into these guys during the Dark Night of the Soul.

What she settled for that Summer struck me as a somewhat unsatisfactory compromise: a Frenchman from a fashionable Manhattan parish whom I judged unfairly to be a total mountebank because, on the strength of my simple-minded countenance (and nothing else, I swear, except perhaps my leg brace), he told Clare solemnly that he thought I had the makings of a saint. When she told me this, I said, "No hagiography for baby," which was her kind of phrase, and she agreed lustily. She was already a better judge of sanctity than Père Pamplemousse (assumed name).

The incident indicates the trouble Clare has always had with the clergy—which is just a genteel variation of the trouble she has had with the world in general. I assumed the poor fellow was simply trying to get in good with her by praising her houseguest, and that he underrated her intelligence a mile. To give the man his due, he caught Harry's just about right, when he lectured Luce later about certain smutty pictures in *Life* and left the great man deeply troubled and vowing to look into it. Little did Pamplemousse wit that the potential saint thought there weren't half enough smutty pictures in *Life*, and was already halfway to the library to see if he'd missed any.

(Incidentally, this account is wholly subjective. I have since learned that the French priest was a good and helpful man, and that only my little-Englander bias made him seem so funny. In fact Clare became quite dependent upon him, and had one of her blackest moods when he was transferred to Australia some years later.)

Clare was not really to make friends with another priest until she met a couple who were semifamous in their own right, John Courtney Murray and Gustav Weigel, S.J. Famous people seem to find each other, not just out of snobbery or even natural superiority, but because they're used to the atmosphere of celebrity and can breathe up there. Humble priests may have to fake it, especially American ones (Europeans would at least know that Clare didn't have a title, and relax accordingly).

For all that, Harry himself seemed to have gotten further along with Catholic theology than our visiting French fireman, who was trying to bring simple Goodness to these very complicated people. Luce once surprised my father, who dropped in now and then, no doubt to see if I was being a nuisance, by confiding precisely why he could never become a Catholic. He had no trouble with the usual hurdles. Infallibility? If anybody understood that one it was Harry. No—it was the True Presence he couldn't accept, the bread that was God. His Presbyterianism, which was deep in his soul, stuck at that. So perhaps there was more to Harry than I gave him credit for. It was also a mistake to think that Goodness could ever be simple for Clare, and the result eventually left her restless and unsatisfied and, as I say, made her feel talentless. But at the time, she was more than content to sacrifice her talent even when she hadn't been asked to. (In fact, converts like Clare can be annoyed at how *little* the Church demands of them.)

Soon after this a simple-goodness screenplay of hers called *Come to the Stable* was produced, and it may, ironically, have finished her as a dramatist to be reckoned with because it included nuns playing softball, which became a period joke. But after World War II, people wanted goodness any way they could get it and at any price. That war, so easily assimilated since, seemed like a million Guernicas at the time—a sign that the human race might possibly be damned. So *all* religious spokesmen tended to stress a moratorium on cleverness. Later Fulton Sheen, who had started out as a philosopher, was particularly taken by the innocence of childhood—so much so that once when he spoke at an old folks' home, a nearby monsignor was heard to mutter, "If he doesn't leave off, he'll have these old people wetting their diapers."

Sheen's distrust of proud, unchildlike intellectuals happened to jibe nicely with conservative dogma about the pin-striped boys at Yalta and Potsdam, and the Luces did their best to accommodate it: or at least to find some really humble intellectuals out there. It was all quite artificial, and it set Clare's writing back to a level of simple ardor that did not come naturally. What she showed me of her attempts that summer was hard to reconcile with *The Women*: but it was her little sacrifice, her juggling before the Virgin. *Come to the Stable* was childish enough for even Bishop Sheen, but that's the chance you take with exorcisms.

Otherwise, religion meant going to Sunday mass and watching Harry kneeling as stiffly as Clarence Day, Sr., in the aforementioned *Life with Father*, while presumably dreaming about the Great Ideas of the West; and Clare very proper and attentive with that half-smile that could mean anything. It was quite in keeping for Harry to link the Catholic Church and the American Century in one powerhouse coalition. But with Clare, you never knew whether she would go along with that or make a little fun of it. The droll voice and face covered all possibilities. And she had something Harry didn't have, namely, irony, and this was reason enough to smile. (Or perhaps Harry was simply staring at the bread on the table, daring it to speak up.)

Sometime around then, the annual novel came out from an embittered ex-staffer lampooning the pair of them. It could have been Ralph Ingersoll's, or it could have been anybody's. Harry was, I gather as usual, totally nonplussed by it. He could not for the life of him see what people found wrong with him. And he was personally hurt. He had an old-school feeling about his employees that very few of them can have shared, and he was especially upset when they brought his wife into it: as if somehow he should, with all his power, have been able to protect her. People who don't think celebrities suffer should have seen Luce knitting his brows over that one.

Clare, on the other hand, seemed quite composed, and even did her best to soothe him. Whether she simply expected no better of life, or whether perhaps, in another incarnation, she could see *herself* satirizing people like Harry and Clare, I can't say. But I did know even then that the theater was her great passion, and that being a dramatist was one thing she had *not* done just to prove she could do it. So it came naturally to her to see herself and Harry as dramatis personae. "Do you find you have different personalities for different people?" she asked me once. I actually thought I didn't back then, which seemed, quite correctly, to tickle her. Even old Harry had at least two personalities.

While she was about it, she told me how to write a play, embroidering on the classic structure: Act I chases the cat up the tree, Act II keeps him there while the crowd gathers, and Act III brings him down again. It didn't help,* any more than the painting equipment she lent me, or the piano in the hall that she claimed she could play like a master (a standard leg-pull. She was quite unmusical, and was even impressed that I could identify some classical standbys like the *Moonlight* Sonata on the Victrola). At eighteen I was already much more suited to retirement than she was. In fact the only practical skill I acquired was learning to drive a car. For this, she volunteered their number two car, a capacious blue Buick with the portholes of the period, which the Swedish chauffeur surrendered somewhat apprehensively; and after hacking my way

---

* But it did worm into my system, because recently I wrote a children's story about a climbing cat, and only afterwards remembered the source.

through the Connecticut tundra, I eventually received a license, from a local cop who had somehow gotten it into his head that I was Fulton Sheen's son.

All this surrounded what was for me the climax of the summer, an incident that perhaps makes me an unreliable witness to everything else. It seems that every year on her late daughter's birthday Clare was in the habit of giving someone a surprise present, and this year the lucky victim was me. On August 22 or thereabouts I was informed that an Oldsmobile 76 was on its way to me from Detroit, under two conditions: (1) that it not contain a radio, since a radio had been playing when her daughter met with the freak accident that killed her, and (2) that I not mention it to anyone. I trust that the statute of limitations has run out on that one. I have not asked her.

A third, unspoken, condition seemed to be that I should not thank her unduly for it. She was quite brisk, even distant, about the whole thing. "You can thank me by kissing me in a crowded place," she said, hitting me in the shyness, "a good old Sheed buss." Finally, I proved too chicken to pay off, and she seemed just a little scornful. But it was never mentioned again, either the car or the kiss.

No doubt whenever a rich person dispenses largess, it can be interpreted as a power play, or a bid for glory (the alternative is to be known as a tightwad). But I cannot see how a gift can be given more cleanly than this one. As the coming years would show, there was certainly no power about it; and as for glory, it is only by chance that I've ever heard of any of her other beneficiaries. I don't suppose she vowed them all to silence as she did me, but that was certainly the idea. The only gift she ever mentioned was to a woman who subsequently made a vitriolic attack on her, and she told me this years later to verify her dictum (since stolen many times) that "no good deed goes unpunished." But of all things she didn't want to be famous for, generosity came surprisingly high: perhaps because it didn't require intelligence, *anyone* could do it.

Extravagance may have been something else. She denies that she actually uttered the famous line, in Tiffany's, "Damn it, Harry, are we rich or aren't we?" but she could have: it was her kind of joke, and Harry was just the man to use it on, being ill at ease in virtually all settings, but also shyly pleased with his royally flamboyant wife. He didn't mind playing the Grumpus husband in their comic strip. She also enjoyed having money, and the enjoyment spilled over. She was especially proud of having invested in *Life* *with Father* and *Oklahoma!,* up to then the longest-running play and musical respectively in Broadway history. This was money made by her own wits and not Harry's or the late George Brokaw's ancestors,* and she was happy to emphasize that. Her feel for theater was, of all her attainments, the most distinctly hers and the least distinctly some helpful man's.

Like most rich people she was besieged by parasites, and had become extremely sensitive to the touch. If I had shown any interest at all in her money, I would certainly never have seen that car. Although I gathered from her secretary that she gave out occasional handouts to old friends down on their luck, it probably helped enormously if they hadn't asked for it. She won't to this day lend money, because people get sore at you when they can't pay it back. So she just gives it—which sometimes makes them even sorer.

In a general way, she seems to feel that helping people materially puts friendship at risk, though she does it anyway. I can't prove that she has never treasured the power of the purse, the freedom to choose and to assert herself that way: it would have been a miracle if she hadn't. People who marry money or otherwise get it through the transom can be especially lordly about its disposition, to make up. But Clare has made enough on her own since Brokaw days to lose that need.

To gauge precisely how tender she felt about being exploited, I would have needed to know a great deal more about her former life than I was able to piece together that summer. She had a way of making stories out of her past, on a varying scale of truthfulness. When she told me that George Brokaw was a mean drunk, that was obviously true, because she said it so flatly. When she said solemnly, "I knew a ballplayer once. His name was Babe Ruth. He came to my mother's house a lot," she was as obviously pulling my leg, though I'm afraid it wasn't obvious right away, as I let out a great yawp of excitement.

But in between was a vast area where fact and fantasy seemed to crisscross. A semi-miracle story about praying for a sign, a red rose as I remember, and receiving it in Congress no less, on the eve of her conversion; tales of her old buddy Winston Churchill and of how he tried to marry her off to his pointless son Randolph ("A man totally unspoiled by failure," she quoted Noël Coward as saying); a particularly gripping account of how Harry had once bab-

---

* George Brokaw was Clare's first husband, who'd inherited a piece of a garment fortune.

bled Mandarin Chinese under ether, although he hadn't spoken the
language since he was twelve—thus revealing to her the Chinese
origins of *Time*-style.

With the half-smile, and the droll voice, they could all have
been put-ons. But at the time, I took them as evidence of an incredi-
bly dramatic life. Outside of the glooms of the Brokaw marriage
and the pain of her daughter's death, it was all Arabian Nights stuff
with an adventure a day, and it fired one's ambition to live likewise,
which may have been the idea.

As a young Socialist sunning myself by the pool, I overlooked
one other important clue to Clare, which is how well she got along
with at least some of her servants. I suppose I would have considered this derisible evidence anyway: if I'd been lucky enough to
have them, I'm sure I would have got along famously with my servants. But it's hard to be fair to the rich. Servants can be a moral
test, and a tough one. A successful executive I know is completely
at the mercy of his old family cook, and eats nearly inedible meals
night after night. And just behind cooks, who can be almost as
temperamental in real life as they are in Wodehouse, you find
housekeepers who job-tested as prison matrons, and drunken gar-
deners, and housemaids who didn't tell you they were pregnant: a
floating gallery of misfits willing to work for less money than other
people in exchange for who knows what.

I didn't, as I say, notice much about how Clare handled this
then, except to observe that she employed a fascinating German
woman as, I guess, lady's maid, though "companion" would have
been closer. This woman was also by chance an epileptic, and Clare
went to considerable lengths to conceal this from Harry. Unfortunately, one night when I wasn't there, Gretel had a seizure right in
the middle of dinner; and Harry, shedding both his kindness and
indifference, could only sputter something like "Get her out of
here, get her out of here," or so it came third-hand to me. I don't
believe that Luce was cruel, only infinitely perturbable, and Gretel
stayed on, although without further public appearances. (Clare
claims that she later saved the poor woman from rape in an Italian
laundromat, and this seems believable. Gretel was spectacularly ill-
fated.)

Outside of the amiable, slightly beery chauffeur, the only
other servant I remember was not a servant at all, but Clare's extraordinary secretary, Dorothy Farmer. Dorothy is still around, a
dear friend, who has asked me to leave her out of this as much as
possible: but her distaste for publicity itself tells a tale, and I'm

afraid I'll have to override it for just a moment, because she's evidence, a sample of the kind of people the daylight Clare likes to have around her.

Dorothy was, and is, a rollicking irreverent character, whose role seemed always to be that of a Sancho Panza to Clare's pretensions. She had joined Clare right after the latter's conversion, and no one could have been a greater contrast to whatever worlds Clare might have left behind her. There must have been ways to disturb Dorothy's humorous equilibrium short of the Second Coming itself, but I can't imagine what they were: certainly nothing in the way of worldly success. So if Clare wanted to fight the demons of ambition, she picked her crony well. If Clare gave an order that struck Dorothy as silly, Dorothy's face showed it at once: not willfully, but because she was a friend and couldn't help it. On reading Clare's plays recently, I note a fascination with outspoken, independent-minded employees, as if she identified with them in some way. And although the plays were written well before she knew Dorothy Farmer, the latter would have been right at home in any of them.

Thus does an author surround herself with her own characters. Clare's interest in quick-witted people of humble origin meant nothing special to me then. I assumed from her name and manner that she herself came from a tony family; and when Harry proclaimed on the way out of *The Great Gatsby* (the Alan Ladd version), "I know what was bothering Scott Fitzgerald—it was the absence of a real aristocracy in America," I gathered he meant the shortage of people like himself and Clare, and how they were undervalued in a Harry Truman world. It never occurred to me that *they* might be the Gatsbys looking for the light across the Sound.

Harry's family did descend on us once in what seemed like unmanageable droves, though it was probably only two or three of them; and I guess they were pretty much what you'd expect from Presbyterian missionary stock—starchy, gray, and formidable; and Clare seemed to semi-retreat from them, as if they owned the place and not she. Harry ceased to be mandarin-like and seemed more like a flustered emissary between Clare and his imperious relatives. Since they presumably disapproved of her (for marrying Harry), they only had to be themselves to seem monstrously disapproving. I had never knowingly met a Presbyterian before, and the Luces didn't bubble with ethnic warmth. So I converted these probably neutral characters to dragons on the spot, and avoided them too, because I belonged to Clare's party in this dispute, and was no doubt viewed as *her* unaccountable property by them. I don't know how much of this was fair and how much my own shyness branching out in fresh directions, because Clare did not speak about it, or about anything else in particular, while they were there, but tells me everything's all right now, and that she gets on splendidly with all the surviving Luces. (She does, too, as far as the eye can see.) Clare hates loose* ends, unnecessary enemies, feuding for its own sake.

The only other Luce I really got to know was Harry's younger son, Peter, who seemed to stand slightly outside the family—not mad enough at anyone to be a rebel, but just different. His attitude seemed to be, don't make plans for me, don't expect any dynasties around here, and everything'll be okay. (Since his elder brother, Hank, looked like Heir Apparent enough for two, nobody seemed to worry about this.) Peter was also the closest thing to the guys I knew on the outside, so we became, for his brief visit, friends. He had his own little airplane, a rickety Piper Cub, and he flew his father and me over the Finger Lakes one day, or some kind of lakes—I'm not dead sure, because I was abysmally airsick in the stuffy, bobbing cabin. I expected Harry to disapprove and shout, "Get him out of here," but he was genuinely solicitous.

Peter was just a few years older than I, so we talked about girls a bit, which on the whole was a mistake, because there didn't seem to be any within miles. Every now and then, Clare would address herself to the problem—"You probably want to meet some girls"—but there it stuck. I seem to remember a niece of some kind coming over for afternoon tea, because Youth meant family, there was no other kind available. Meanwhile, my driving instructor, an ex-marine, would comment at exhaustive length on every woman we passed, probably to calm his nerves as I wobbled along; and the boys in the barbershop talked about poontang on Saturday afternoons, until I could stand no more. The Party was just about over. My car hadn't arrived yet and I was too young to order the chauffeur to drive me to the nearest bar; too young, really, to be here at all. It was amazing that I hadn't noticed that before.

Clare herself did not seem trapped, but came and went casually. Ridgefield seemed like a good town to be famous in—at any rate, it was used to her. And she sometimes drove around it herself,

* The pun question has to be faced sometime. Being a "Luce woman," for instance, is one of those minor irritations, probably no easier to take if you've once been a booth or a broker.

though her eyesight seemed shaky, and her driving, well, *different*, or was driven, on the usual errands of life, without being gawked at unduly. I have since wondered, though, whether both her apparent serenity and her alleged haughtiness came from slight myopia: from knowing she was looked at, but not quite seeing back. (She says "no," but I'm attached to my theory.)

The limits of her kind of freedom became clear one evening when we went to a small country inn, in a sizable group, to eat dinner. "Uh oh," said Clare, "watch out for trouble." There was only one other party present, and in my unworldliness I didn't recognize the recessive chin and birdlike gaze of the woman. But sure enough, a day or so later, Dorothy Kilgallen reported in her column that she had seen Clare having an intimate, candlelight supper alone with George Waldo. The rest of us had evaporated.

Later I was to learn that you didn't even have to be with Clare to be invisible—sitting in her car was enough. That fall, I was driven to the premiere of *Come to the Stable,* and I still recall the disappointed groans of the groupies as I stepped out of the limousine alone, in my ill-fitting dinner jacket. The public can look imbecilic and menacing in the glare of flashbulb and neon, and I see why actors hide from it and writers fantasize riots. But the worst of it, really, is the way they reduce Fame to random staring and pawing. The people who hang around zoos to see the animals copulate must wear the same expressions.

To think you fought your way up the tree to the Golden Apple, to find a half-wit staring at you ... Anyway, it had long since ceased being fun for Clare, if it ever was (that's why I was alone in the car—she was being smuggled through a back door), and was just a nagging inconvenience. It meant having less than nimble-witted people come up to your table at "21" to express their admiration at grueling length. And it meant these same people cutting you off from your friends—because fans are maniacally possessive and proportionately brutal to the unfamous. I have seen celebrities' wives virtually used as hat racks at parties where their husbands are being lionized. And the same thing happens to anyone who hangs out with superstars. Only after the star has left the table will the fan turn his mad, gleaming eyes on you to say, "You know her well? What's she really like? Are *you* somebody?"

If ever Clare had courted this kind of adulation, she wasn't courting it now. Without making a Garbo-like fuss about it, she simply avoided these situations as much as possible. It made for a circumspect life, which is a handicap for a writer/observer. Even

Norman Mailer, who can perform prodigies of anonymity by shrinking his personality at will, as if his aura were collapsible, must frequently wish that the basic face were less well known. With Clare the problem was incalculably worse. Nothing short of heavy disguise would have hidden those features, after which she would have had the usual problems of unaccompanied females anyway. And Harry, I feel strongly, would not really have cared to have her going round dressed as an Apache dancer or a German governess, though she was corny and mischievous enough to do it.

So her range of vision was limited to people she knew and trusted. Up to then, that might not have hampered her too much. She carried a wide range of recent memories from the days before fame set in. And her interest in her servants and in flotsam like me made up in intensity whatever she might be losing in scope. She had an immense curiosity about people, and particularly about any comedy that might attach to them. In those days, *Time* ran a column called "Miscellany," full of the sort of dotty small-town items that English newspapers relish and that our own Bob and Ray would pick up and run with, and Clare was constantly scouting for it. Her conversation was and is also peppered with such stories, which were curiously bound up with her romance with America.

Largely against my wishes, the summer ended, and I have never passed another remotely like it. I spent a couple of nights in the deluxe Luce suite at the Waldorf to acclimatize myself to the harshness of city living. Harry insisted that I use his barber, which might have been preying on his mind for some time, and I got the worst $7.50 haircut in history, on the house. Harry also uttered one of my favorite lines, "You don't eat roast lamb in restaurants," which left me wondering where you *did* eat it, since I'd never seen any at his place.

Finally, he told me all about Sports, which he had just discovered and which he now saw as central to human life and well-being, though he had previously found them a waste of time. Naturally, there would be a magazine in this. He was at special pains to explain to me my ruling passion, baseball. It seems that the game is so perfect that people get their kicks waiting for errors. I responded meekly that although I had never personally known anyone who waited for errors, I would certainly think it over. "Whut, whut?" he said.

That was about the last I saw of Harry. I suppose he must have noticed I wasn't there one day, but I suspect he shrugged it off

briskly as one of those things. Life was too full of small, inexplicable events to track them all down.

I realize that I have presented Luce so far as pretty much a
clown. He was, of course, much more than that, and his impact on
Clare's life was anything but clownish. But he was that, too, or
seemed so to me, and it made him oddly likable. Very oddly. If one
bears in mind Clare's taste for the comic, their marriage makes a
little more sense: she wasn't just marrying power, she was marrying
a splendid joke.

And her tacit amusement over it robbed him of much of his
terrors. Whether he was grilling me about the Catholic theology of
voluntary acts, or the nature of the Dred Scott decision (two discussions that float to mind), one sensed her levity counterbalancing his
earnestness; not precisely making fun of him, but more in a spirit of
"Well, there goes Harry."

Before I left, there was one more dinner, which could almost
have been a Pan American board meeting. I found myself sitting
next to Sam Pryor, vice-president of that company, and I wish I'd
paid more attention, because it was he who gave Clare her first big
nudge toward Congress, and it was, as we shall see, this Pan
American connection that explains some of her policy there. But all
I can remember is a comfortable, old-shoes sort of fellow, who
made me realize that once you get to the very top, you can afford to
relax, if you still know how.

And talking of old shoes: I had been forced to get into my disgraceful dinner jacket for the occasion, and I won't say I was wearing brown shoes with it, and I won't say I wasn't. In either case,
such shoes as they were resisted any last-ditch attempt to shine
them; and these, along with a sloping, hand-tied bow tie, left me
looking like a burlesque comedian about to whip a salami out of his
pants.

Before joining the power elite in the dining room, I was in-
spected by Clare: after all, I was her responsibility. She was in this
thing too. Maybe there was a fire escape I could use. . . . After a
moment, she said, "I'm very proud of you," and kissed me on the
cheek, and we went in together.

That evening was the last I was to see of Clare for a long, long
time. If I hadn't seen her again, the episode would still be complete.
Just as there are children's books there are children's people—people who might or might not mean something to you later, but were
just right that particular year—and she belongs securely to my pan-

theon, along with a witch called Carryl Houselander and Father
Felix the baseball nut, and so on. Demonologists may have trouble
picturing this with Clare. Celebrities who are "good with children"
usually depress the hell out of actual children. But recently my then
twelve-year-old daughter met Clare and reported that she had
never encountered a more attentive adult: and this prodigious
achievement cannot be faked. Clare Luce seems to have the unique
distinction of being interested in other people's children.

From her own reminiscences, I conjecture that she still identifies with them a little, like comic servants and other clever outsid-
ers, staring through the window at the stuffed shirts, making faces,
feeling a little envy perhaps; and then, my goodness, seeing herself
in there doing famously. It is a playwright's dream.

# CHAPTER THREE

# Coming Down, and Meeting the Legend

It took a while to get used to trudging down the hall to the family bathroom, and waiting for it to empty; going out for the newspaper; making one's own breakfast. After my summer at the Luces', the Ritz itself would have seemed tacky and ill run.

The place we lived that year was the far extreme from the Luces': it was at the wrong end of an undistinguished street, and the only kind of news it was capable of making occurred later in the year when a severed leg was left in a suitcase on our doorstep (a Chinese laundryman had run amuck and scattered limbs all over the neighborhood).

Without making a big deal out of it, my parents absolutely refused to spend unnecessary money on themselves so long as there was one empty rice bowl in India. So I wearily reacquainted myself with the New York City cockroach and light chains that came off in your hand. The Luces faded away rapidly, because there was nothing to connect them with. For a while, their chauffeur brought me their discarded jigsaw puzzles, and I can still picture the poor fellow threading his way incredulously past the garbage cans, to park the Cadillac in front of our ramshackle building. Then even these visits ceased. Perhaps the chauffeur couldn't take it.

From then on, I followed the Luces at a distance, if at all. Outside of occasional bulletins from my parents, who were lecturing nomads in those days (they had once supported their publishing habit by playing the Catholic circuit, which girdled the globe) and saw everybody at least twice a year, all my Luce reports were filtered through the Legend. And very different they seemed from the outside. Almost too different to be true.

"You went to stay with *who?*"

I had shyly revealed what I did on my vacation to my best friend—not to impress him, God knows, but because it seemed like a tough secret to keep to myself all winter. I had expected, and might even have welcomed, a cheerful raspberry for stepping out of my class. What I hadn't counted on was the mild derision, which later would swell to livid disgust, almost every time I mentioned the name Luce in liberal New York. They were the enemy, in a way the goatish Joe McCarthy would never be: because true diabolism takes brains.

I had never really taken in how the liberal Left felt about Clare and at first I thought there must be some mistake. As a vague British Labourite, hell-bent for National Health, subsidized transit, and an end to colonial adventures, I considered myself comfortably to the left of anything in my crowd. So to learn that I had been supping with the devil all summer made me wonder what I had missed.

Try as I could, I could not magnify my recent hosts into national menaces. They never *said* anything menacing, or even top secret. They were not, in my presence anyway, particularly partisan—in fact, on several positions I'd have had trouble identifying which wing they were supposed to be on. But to meet celebrities before you've really heard of them is to be stuck at the wrong end of the telescope. From there I could see Harry playing tennis stiffly or taking his constitutional dip, with that gray no-nonsense torso cleaving the water like an ironing board, before grappling with the evening's idea. Perhaps he seemed a little childish to have so much power, but no more than you'd expect from a press lord.

Still, there wasn't enough *to* Harry as I experienced him to put up against the caricature. He certainly wasn't an ogre, but he was, to an eighteen-year-old stranger, so emotionally impenetrable, it was hard to say *what* he was, outside of that. He had been a boss for so long that he looked like one even in his pajamas. And when he unbent, it was unmistakably a boss unbending. Since he had never worked for anyone else, he had no memory of comradeship in the ranks. So if you were an equal, he could think of nothing to do with you except interview you.

Harry's hedgehog façade made "the Luces" seem more ominous than they really were—though to me there was nothing "Luces" about them. I had no trouble separating them immediately and throwing Luce to the wolves. A more mature observer, who met them both a little later that same year, wrote: "He handsome, well-mannered [!], well-dressed, densely stupid. She exquisitely elegant, clever as a monkey, self-centered." And again: "I found him ignorant and densely stupid. Her I admired for chic and sharpness, but she complained to others that I lacked heart." Honors even, as we say in England.*

The speaker is, of course, Evelyn Waugh, and it is worth noting that the great satirist had no trouble at all in telling the Luces apart. To him they were almost different in kind. Although he takes one or two routine swipes at Clare later on in his letters and diaries, it is clear from the second annotation that he rather wished her approval, not an everyday occurrence for Waugh. And in the winter of '49, grumbling all the way, he actually gave a big party for her in London, which he thought went very well. (It must be admitted that Clare's Catholicism did not hurt a bit with old prickle puss.)

Waugh's insults frequently lack the precision of his compliments and his cracks about Harry sound suspiciously like his cracks about Americans in general. But insofar as there was a subject involved, it crisscrossed with my own difficulties with Luce. Harry was enlisting Waugh for one of his "really big" projects: a picture-book history of all of Western culture. Waugh found it childish, philistine, richly comic. Clare, who might well have approved the project herself, would have learned instantaneously from the Master's somewhat overdone derision (he scorned *all* mass education). Harry would not have if you gave him all afternoon. In this respect he *was* a bit stupid, not worthy to be a Luce.

And as I thought about it more, I couldn't deny, as I once had, a link between Harry's personal style and his magazines' politics. Few Americans can have had so little experience of day-to-day democracy as Luce. In China, it had been all masters and servants, mandarins and peasants, preachers and natives. As a colonial transplant at Hotchkiss and Yale, it was prizes and getting tapped

---

* *The Letters of Evelyn Waugh,* ed. Mark Amory. (New York: Ticknor & Fields), pp. 288–89.

for bones and *winning* your inequality fair and square. In marriage, it was, as Fitzgerald would say, getting the top girl.

This was the America he loved, the land of the self-made mandarin; but of the other side of America, the side that just gets by, or doesn't, and that doesn't want to compete or go places, but just to put its feet up, he knew practically nothing. (He once said that he had no time for anyone who slept past 9 A.M., a view that Clare's sleeping habits may have modified.) Anyway, all he needed was a nice, noncompetitive wife like Clare to complete his isolation from rocking chair America—which may have contributed to the wide-eyed quality of *Life*, which was always simply beside itself about that America.

I have since noted that the people who knew Harry seem to like him a little bit more each year that he isn't with us, often at the expense of Clare's end of the seesaw. I know what they mean: the mannerisms now seem endearing, like an old teacher's, once he can no longer harm you. Yet at the time, no one I met seemed comfortable with Luce. The phrase "he had no small talk" achieved formidable proportions in his case; and he was never more disconcerting than when he tried to make up for this by swarming over small talk, trying to master in one session the details that normally absorbed Clare: the cook's last name, the average height of chauffeurs, how people lived and what they thought.

In this phase, he would make an unholy fuss about things that didn't concern him in the least, as if this were an editor's solemn duty. His famous yearning for a hometown struck me as purest journalistic malarkey. He'd have been bored stiff by a hometown, if his interest in Ridgefield was anything to go by, or his choice of a nice average American girl to marry. Clare and he seemed equally but oppositely outside the everyday America they championed, for their own very good reasons.

None of this seemed to qualify Luce ideally to run such omniscient magazines. That summer he read George Orwell's *1984* and was even more than normally disturbed by it. And it struck me that he just didn't know whether the human race was like that, or could be like that, and that he would thus be fair game for *any* prophet with the right line of blarney. Oddly enough, despite the Hiss case, I cannot remember more than a passing mention of Whittaker Chambers at Luce's place, and I doubt if Harry could have cared much personally for that slovenly antithesis of a power person. I do dimly recall his annoyance that Chambers had deceived *him* about his communist past, as if this were the worst of the pumpkin man's offenses. But by then Chambers' apocalypse-mongering had already played to Luce's weakness, so that we had all that organ music about the decline of the West, coming from booming Rockefeller Center where the West looked to be doing just fine. The decline of the West was a big story, and he loved a big story. In the end, I believe that his habit of shaping things into news stories was the real wall between him and reality.

On the plus side, I remember feeling that Luce did believe in Virtue, again in a schoolboy way, but genuinely and with vigor and he was probably less cynical than Clare—perhaps too much less. (That was then. I now think of them bisecting cynicism and each taking half.) He was not, as I recall, obsessed with enemies in the stereotyped right-wing manner, but only with his beloved American Century,* which he was trying to conduct like a one-man band. I didn't think America was ready for a century, at least until *Time-Life* stopped snapping its gum like that, and those really *were* his magazines, no matter how demure he was about it: in fact, they looked more like their daddy every day, once you knew him.

So I conceded Harry to the liberals, on those momentous occasions when I thought about him at all. He was enough like his legend to pass. And besides, his real life was probably not in that house that summer: I had been tip-toeing around a courtly wax-works, who lacked a home as much as a hometown. What I couldn't see was the continued and unflickering distaste for *Clare*. By now she was almost invisible, and had not pushed, backbitten, or crashed a headline in years. But even in a convent, she would have been part of "the Luces," manacled to her husband in one of our great national acts. Although she claimed her marriage had actually cost her one of our great publicity resources—*Time* magazine scarcely ever mentioned her, though *Life* made up for it some—it was seen as a self-generating, perpetual-motion power play. So she didn't have to do *anything* to give offense.

Since it was now in perfect repose, Clare's legend could be studied like a Grecian urn, with her forever reaching or being reached for, depending on one's angle of vision. Her admirers seemed as frozen in place as her critics. They were happy to celebrate her conversion, or her achievements as a Woman, or her spunky duels with FDR, in perpetuity. If she had gone out of exis-

---

* He had used this phrase in a *Life* editorial in 1938 in specific reference to nazism and communism, but Henry Wallace dug it up in 1942, suggesting that it meant U.S. imperialism, and Luce was hung with it. Rough justice for the old pamphleteer.

tence like St. Christopher, they'd have kept her on their dash-
boards.

I had never fully realized before this how personal legends
harden into statues, at which point the originals can go on about
their business and let the statues mind the store. What puzzled me
here was how the statue could be so unlike the woman I met. Was
this true about all the statues in the garden, or was Clare a special
case? It was like finding that that nice woman on the train was
Catherine de Médicis.

Looking for clues was rather like grilling Dr. Watson or Mortimer Snerd. The prejudice for and against her was, like most prejudices, as vague as it was sure of itself. Sometimes people had a
secondhand story to tell about her (often the same one), in which
Clare lectures the Pope or terrorizes Tiffany's, just as racists get by
on one anecdote. But frequently they had no stories at all. She just
had to be awful, that's all. That kind of woman was always awful.
Or wonderful.

Well, what kind of woman? Not my Mr. Chips of the Summer,
nor even the slightly solemn show-off of the dinner table. Someone
else, a concoction, a mask. Her career had activated the public's
need to hate, along with its need to grovel, and I became fascinated
with the mechanics of this, as I would later be with Muhammad
Ali, a similar case, at least in that respect.

Since I didn't see her for years and I did hear the legend played
over and over, I came to know the latter intimately, and even to
dislike it myself, because that was obviously its purpose. The icy
blond, bright, greedy, insensitive—who could like such a person? It
was as if the celebrity world existed to spin out moral fables, of
haughty queens and humble haberdashers, Clare Luces and Harry
Trumans, for our constant instruction, and these fables become
dogma. "She's really a nice woman," I would say: and a quick sur-
vey of eyebrows would tell me, he's showing off again, pretending
to know something. Mae West is really chaste, oh sure. If there's
one thing we know for certain, it's our celebrities.

So I stopped defending my friend (which she had warned me
would be a waste of time, before I knew it would even arise) and
took to meditating on reputation as such and on how Clare drew
her particular part in the national morality play. Her early career
still existed for me as a scatter of photographs and tags of dialogue:
Clare in uniform, Clare on the platform, etc., with captions by her.
Only years later, in 1977, did I sit down with Clare as we had in the
old days, except that we were somehow transposed to Hawaii, to fit

some of the pieces together. "Does my life mean anything at all?" she says, smiling; i.e., are we working on another Matisse or does this one tell a story?

A word of warning about what follows: if Clare has ever gotten a date right, outside of her birthday and certain national emergencies, I've missed it. Thus it has been pointed out by Helen Lawrenson (in a curious essay* on Clare that I'll get around to later) that if you followed every written account of Clare, you would have her going to three schools, in widely different parts of the country, at one and the same time. Since I can find no special point to these distortions or several others like them (unless Clare was entering a claim for bilocation), I can't put them *all* down to self-glorification.

In a rare burst of charity Ms. Lawrenson concedes that Clare might have had such a wretched childhood that her imagination had to embroider it. Perhaps. But this would not explain why Clare has also been known to embroider the events of last week, when the mood is on her. Like many writers (perhaps even Lawrenson in her weaker moments), Clare seems to feel that almost any story can use a little touching up before one inflicts it on an audience. By chance the schools she mentioned to me check out—I've seen the class photos—but this next will not be a chapter about schools, or about whether Clare really spent her summers in Wisconsin. It is simply a meditation on a career: or to use a phrase proper to the years when it happened, what a smart girl had to do to get ahead in the Twentieth Century. There will be no unseemly straining after objectivity. Harry wouldn't have liked it.

* Helen Lawrenson, "The Woman," *Esquire*, August, 1974.

# CHAPTER FOUR

# *Notes on a Career - I: Clare Solo, 1903-39*

Clare did not really have an American hometown any more than Harry, although she didn't carry on about it as he did. ("When you're in America, you're simply in America," she says, adding, "especially in Hawaii.") Technically she seems to have been born in New York City, America's waiting room, on April 10, 1903. She actually did have a stage mother, as well as a legitimate stage name. Her mother was one Anna Clara Snyder, an actress, and her own last name, she says, was shared by an ancestor called John Wilkes Booth, a man who also hung around theaters.

It is a neat connection, Clare and John: two theatrical snipers, who combined drama and politics with combustible effects. It is very much her kind of story, with the kind of symmetry she looks for and suspiciously often finds. If she were writing an autobiography, it would probably team with coincidences, juxtapositions, droll outcomes.

Her Grandfather Boothe, who was a Baptist pastor, added the *e*, she says, to distance his family at once from the assassin, but it was a clumsy disguise. A good third of my correspondents still spell "Boothe" wrong and I, being a lifelong fumble-spell, have to look it up even now. Passing unnoticed is not a family trait.

Pastor Boothe used to give a particularly powerful sermon

38

The Boothe inheritance: preacher vs. showman. The family gathered at White Plains: Clare's grandparents (far right) and father (next to column, center)

Clare's father, William "Billy" Boothe (left, his obituary picture; right, as a younger man)

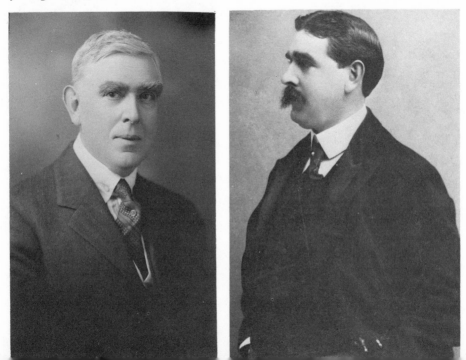

"Thought" to be Billy,
the phantom fiddler

Anna Clara Snyder

Brother
and sister

The graduate

Brother David,
1941

Clare's first news story:
the great train crash near
Bullsville, New York, 1911

Reconnoitering Europe, 1914

Invading. The second European trip, 1920

With Dr. and Mrs. Alfred Austen, 1922

George Brokaw by day

George Brokaw by night

Clare with Ann

Managing Editor, *Vanity Fair*, in caricature and by Cecil Beaton

Sitting it out with Baruch,
Mepkin, South Carolina

The Luces at play (late 30's)

Humoring Conde Nast

During second Congressional campaign, 1944

Clare and Harry with Jo Davidson, the sculptor: Harry slightly out of it, but proud as punch

Clare with Dorothy Thompson, between bouts

Gertrude Stein, Clare, and Harry

Wilkie and fellow Bernard Shaw fan, Gene Tunney

For once, ill at ease: Clare with fellow congresswomen

Clare and Mme. Chiang, short-arms drill

With the Chiangs and General Stilwell

"A U.S. division can do anything"—Truscott (G.I. cast of *The Women*)

"THE WOMEN"

The serious side of war: at the front with the Fifth Army, 1944

Clare with
daughter Ann

Clare and the bird
(c. 1939)

against the theater, which had the time-honored effect of making his children stagestruck. As if to illustrate the curious attraction/repulsion toward the stage in this family, a shadowy daughter named Laura was shot to death in a New York hotel in 1898, by herself or other, while serving a stint as a light comedienne at the Gaiety Theater. Her husband was the acting company manager.

The story illustrates Parson Boothe's rare gift for estrangement. The original news clip refers to Laura as *"thought* to be the daughter of" (my italics), which suggests that even her memory had been erased. She is also named alternately "Booth" and "Boothe." Dr. Boothe, after reluctantly acknowledging that she was indeed his daughter, resigned his ministry a month later, aged sixty. So when Clare refers to her young self as cut off from the Boothes one needn't imagine a slight chill in the air but one of those sundering Victorian things. The effect of these was often not to hold families together but to send them sprawling like marbles. William Boothe, Clare's father, was an aspiring fiddler who left home early and often—first his father's, then his wife's—flitting across Clare's screen almost too fast to be an influence, except in the general sense of adding a slap of greasepaint to the image. Because, with his father's sermon ringing in his ears, he inevitably wound up playing his fiddle in the orchestra pit and marrying one of the show girls. And if Clare was not exactly born in a prop box, the show girl Boothe married—Clare's mother Anna Clara Snyder (Ann Clare for everyday use)—could at least make much melodrama out of an absent husband and just about anything else that came along.

Clare's family memories are appropriately misty, as if memory itself were a camera of the period. In fact, Mr. Boothe seems almost a negative. Although he was not officially divorced until 1913, he was always skittering off someplace, so that when he occasionally reappeared it was like a face at the window. Clare talks of meeting him again as a stranger on a train, but her age seems to change each time I hear it (*Let me see, that must have been in . . . no, wait a second*), so that the anecdote has a literally dreamy quality about it like *Alice Through the Looking-Glass.* Thus, as she tells it, her reaction to the man on the train has a bit of the startled child about it, and a bit of the cool woman. In dreams, she may have met him at every age. People with disappearing fathers are prone to fantasies about them, though I'm sure that there was a father and there was a train and that she could pin it down if anyone was dull enough to insist on it. I even believe that this elfin fiddler ran a Coca-Cola bottling plant in Memphis which Clare visited one summer, and started a music company, and anything else I hear about him: the moonstruck young man in the family photograph was capable of *starting* anything. But the only thing lasting about Billy Boothe's legacy is that he encouraged young Clare to read and learn languages. If he hadn't, nobody else would have.

Most of her early memories are clearer than that, and if one allows for the *Looking-Glass* chronology, not particularly contradictory. She *was* poor. Mr. Boothe, an indifferent provider on his best day, finally gave up altogether and left his wife and two infants, Clare and David, high and dry—although in letters he wrote near the end of his life (which enraged their mother) he claimed to have supported them all along. "He couldn't have sent us much," says Clare, citing the near-tenement they lived in on Columbus Avenue when she was young, where she remembers bathing in the kitchen sink, to a smell of cabbage.

Her mother, the former chorus girl, was the granddaughter of a stable owner (social equivalent of a trucking garage) in Hoboken, which meant solid enough German-American stock. But the Snyder family was depleted by the now-curable illnesses of the period—T.B., spinal meningitis, and so on—and what was left of it did not hit it off with the Protestant Boothes anyway. Even without the dreaded show-biz connection, an interfaith marriage would have meant automatic ostracism (now, Clare says, "you're happy if they just marry anybody"), so Ann Snyder Boothe suddenly had nothing to go on except good looks and a fanatical belief in the American dream ("Up the ladder, *up* the ladder"), which she injected into her son and daughter in killer doses, with drastically opposite results. The first words they heard were of success; the first lesson they learned was suspicion.

It goes without saying that a woman in Ann Clare's position depended a good deal on the friendship of men, up to the limit imposed by middle-class appearances, which reigned above even money or love. (C.: "I don't know about *her* morals, but I had to be pure.") The family standard of living presumably bumped up and down to the tune of mother's courtships, and Clare allows that there were several. For the most part the suitors were just part of the scenery, not, as Clare describes it, the great shaking traumas they would be to children in novels. But one particular man almost qualified as a steady boyfriend and was perhaps Clare's greatest indirect benefactor, a rough but kindly Jewish tire merchant called Joseph Jacobs.

It was Jacobs who administered the lesson that would later

evolve into the moral of *The Women,* although I gather this form of it is a bit of a chestnut in Jewish families. It seems that Joe liked to tell a story about a man called Ike, who encouraged his son to jump into his arms from various heights with cries of "Trust me, trust me," until when full confidence was established, he dropped the wretched lad. "You see, you gotta be suspicious of everybody," Ike explains to his crushed offspring.

The two fatherless kids did not need this particular piece of advice right then, and burst into tears at the story, to their mother's bewilderment. Instead of comforting them, she scolded them for crying, while Jacobs scratched his head, the most bewildered of them all.

Jacobs was to learn his own lesson, though perhaps he already knew it. Although his support of the family was unflagging in every pinch, and Ann Clare seems to have been as devoted to him as she could be, she flatly refused to marry him. "I can't," she told the children, "I can't have a Jewish father for my children. They'll never get anywhere." Reeling from her own rejection by Congregationalists, Ann Clare was taking no chances.

Years later, Bernard Baruch may have turned the tables on Clare, as we shall see, but right then these were the rock facts of snobbery, and Jacobs seems to have accepted them. Ann Clare regarded herself as potential royalty, which meant, to her operatic soul, a proper marriage and a heartbreaking affair. When she finally did marry a respectable Protestant named Dr. Albert Austin, the groom found himself playing pinochle nightly with Joseph Jacobs. The doctor knew the score too, and Jacobs remained part of the family until Ann Clare and he died together in a stalled car on a railroad track in 1938. The once penniless Mrs. Boothe left $5 million in her will, although by then nobody needed it.

An untidy sort of life, for those who have never had to do it, but one comically ennobled in Ann Boothe's case by her crazy dedication. Her children were going to make it somehow or other. In 1913 she took the ten-year-old Clare to Europe on a shoestring (she actually said it was to save money), to dip the child quickly into culture and make a fair lady of her before the Kaiser could intervene. Clare believes that her mother met Jacobs the provider on board ship and Jacobs proposed on the spot. If so, one might surmise that project Clare was launched then and there.

If one imagines Clare's mother as a flinty-eyed schemer at this point, one has at least the eyes wrong. What they were most of the time was moist. Ann Clare was hopelessly romantic, a victim of too

many operettas and all-round *Gemütlichkeit*. She wept like a faucet
at the slightest provocation, at which times all her woes were ora-
torically regurgitated, but this sounds more entertaining than menacing and the only trace it left on Clare was a determination never
to cry in front of her own daughter, a decision she now regrets. But
there was no inhibition on laughter, and Clare remembers the
household fairly rocking with it as her slightly manic-depressive
mother barreled through the day. Clare remembers her childhood as
more happy than not—and even if this is slightly wishful remembering, there must have been enough happiness to fuel even that.

The effects on her slightly elder brother were less fortunate,
not because of any personal friction that Clare can remember, but
because there was no role for a boy in Ann Clare's game plan. As a
punishment, she dressed David up in girl's clothes on at least one
occasion and said, "See—you're a girl, you're a girl": a piece of period barbarism that symbolizes precisely how much she was at sea
with a son. "You're just like your father," she told him whenever he
did something wrong. (And if you act like him, we may have to
turn you into a girl again.) She wasn't cruel, just befuddled. She
couldn't simply plunge David into museums and concert halls and
show him off on shipboard. The two women could improvise a life,
but there was only one way a successful boy could grow up in those
days. Straight as string.

I am bringing up David first because *Clare* brought him up first
over lunch in Hawaii as we began to poke through the wastebaskets
of memory. It was obviously some sort of necessary preface.

Not surprisingly, young David developed minor disciplinary
problems. Spending one's nights in a gypsy encampment and one's
days in the rigid schools of the period, one finds it hard to strike the
right note. According to a source that may or may not be reliable,
David did some petty thieving off bakery trucks and such for the
common good. And one imagines a Robin Hood anarchy welling
up that could be embarrassing in better times. The solution chosen
for this was unfortunately that cliché of the period, military school.
If a boy needed love (a strange boy indeed), he would at least get
over the need there. And if he had emotional problems, discipline
should flatten those out in no time.

Perhaps the system did work in some cases, though it had the
besetting handicap of prisons in general, i.e., that all the inmates
were in the same boat, and couldn't help each other much. But with
David, the apprenticeship also put him completely out of sync with
his soaring sister, already sampling Paris with a governess and

hoping to be an understudy on Broadway. In a cruel reversal of the usual Victorian alignment, the boy felt grounded while the girl prepared to go places. Career Woman I, a prototype, was being lovingly groomed while he was simply being whipped into shape. And he couldn't even claim to feel cheated, because it was made quite clear that the family money was paying his school bills, while Clare's trip was an economy. So he drilled and she had her first croissant at the Pension Balzac, still fondly remembered.

David ran away from school at age sixteen to join the Marines in time to find himself fighting at Belleau Wood: the first of two such escapes that gave shape to his life. The possibility that Ann had sent the wrong kid to school doesn't seem to have dawned on anyone.

Clare talks with enormous wistfulness of her brother. Although the imperatives of success and the American Dream pulled them apart, they were also co-conspirators under the skin, as fatherless children can sometimes be, with a private emotional language. She still feels peeved with him over sixty-five-year-old incidents: a time she came to his defense and he resented it, and a time when he *didn't* come to hers, in routine small-fry confrontations concerning such matters as pigtail pulling.

The precise quality of their friendship is illuminated by their adult behavior, so we'll jump nimbly over time, like Clare herself, and take a quick look at that. Although Clare has at times been accused (by the ever-helpful Ms. Lawrenson among others) of being a social climber with a corrected nose, accent, and the trimmings, she never tried to hide David, who remained defiantly uncorrected, with a street accent and style. He may have embarrassed her at times, but everyone got to meet him. So she was no ordinary social climber.

Over the years she also tried to get Brokaw, Baruch, and Luce respectively to launch David in business, and each time it fizzled. One imagines the humiliation of taking help from these superachievers, and then crowning it by letting them down. Tactful Harry above all could not conceal his distaste for this perennial failure of a brother-in-law and was brusque even by his standards, when David came calling. (Actually, as I knew all too well, Harry's normal expression was one of mild distaste, so you had to deduce how you were doing by figuring how you *should* be doing. People thought Harry disliked them when Harry didn't even know they were in the room.) On the archetypal level, for David to fail with the very men that his sister had succeeded with so royally must have been shattering. David could only retaliate, "with bubbling humor, which I don't have." ("Harry doesn't know it," bubbled David once, "but he paid for this suit.")

Clare feels that David was her mirror opposite, failing as systematically as she succeeded. "He had the same weakness as I did for picking things up and dropping them," she says; only what was charming in a woman was feckless in a man. (And how would *she* have done in a military school?) Women were prized precisely for their versatility and frowned on if they showed the monomaniac concentration of successful men. A female Harry Luce would have been considered grotesque. So, too, a male Clare. Then again, although the final thrust has always been her own, each of Clare's careers was launched initially with the help of a man. And David had the same trouble—except that in his case it was wrong. A man who got ahead the way Clare did would have been considered a cad.

David presumably heard the same lessons as Clare, but they came from a woman and were directed at a woman. (Perhaps that's why she put David in a dress—so she'd know what to say to him.) He was taught about success, but with no appropriate instructions. Ann Clare preached, but much more, she acted out what a woman had to do. But David's absent father could only teach him how to disappear.

It adds perspective, as one ticks off Clare's triumphs, to picture David watching on the sidelines, trying to get into the game, ending up with a mouthful of grass. He had resented her coming to his defense as a child, not realizing that this was a pathetic preview of their life, because he never really left her orbit and he always needed help.

There was no point in a half-successful career for David after such a pep talk of a childhood: heading up a business was the least one could do, as Clare's brother, and as Harry's brother-in-law. So he would try, among other things, to run a movie chain and to be a wheel on the stock market. When each business venture failed, one simply tried another, as if there were no humbler possibilities to consider.

Like many such dislocated souls, David Boothe did find something he was good at in World War II. A man with drive but no particular interests can always fight, and war provides a great, vague outlet for random energies, like a golf driving range. So David Boothe became a crack pilot in World War II—the warrior that Clare might have wanted to be herself; his one triumph. Unfortunately, even in this he needed Clare's help, because he was shading forty. "Kid," he said one day, "you're as thick as thieves with Mac-Arthur. Get me into this war," which was one of her easier assignments. David flew hospital planes for a while, and was commissioned in the field for it, and later he flew pursuits with distinction.

Unfortunately, a job that encouraged and fostered rage only served to show how much of it David had, and he began to experience intense black moods which culminated, to his horror, in his beating up a Japanese in the street. Who can measure the frustration of such a man? Peace meant failure. War had brought him the success he burned for, or had been taught to burn for. A gentle, charming man deep down, who "liked to play with children while I [Clare] pontificated," he had found his taste of the American Dream in a warplane, squeezing a trigger. MacArthur offered him a permanent staff job, but he backed off because of the rage problem. So he slipped away from even the thing he was good at.

One day he phoned Clare and signed off as follows: "You're a good kid. [He always called her "Kid."] Remember me in your prayers." The next thing she heard of him was that he had taken his plane out to sea and crashed it, in a way that could just conceivably have been accidental. This was in September 1948—the year before I met Clare and found her so seemingly carefree.

Clare lives with her ghosts as uneasily as most of us. Her life, as the saying goes, amuses her when she thinks about it, but hurts when she feels. (Am I alone in experiencing just the opposite?) In talking about David she says more than once that her own life just doesn't add up—a piece of sisterly solidarity, perhaps. Why should her success mean more than David's failure? It was just a game anyway.

The woman who made up the game for them, Clare's mother, is a gentler memory, and Clare discusses her cheerfully and often. Yet she tells me she has a box of letters from both her mother and her daughter that she doesn't dare open, in case she has "forgotten something." So these are not new shadows; they were there, in varying lengths, on the glory days, too. The cocky Clare that everyone remembers had troubles to burn.

Old-timers still tend to think of Clare as a child actress, and psychologically they're right. She did try literally to be one in her early teens, but according to her, failed abysmally, being easily the worst natural talent in the West. Her mother took her to a screen test in the then film capital of Fort Lee, New Jersey; but whatever kind of actress Clare might have been, it wasn't silent. She did by chance make one stage appearance in a play called *The Dummy.* She understudied Mary Pickford briefly in a play called *A Good Little Devil* without, blessedly, having to appear, and she played "the girl over the fence" in a very short film called *The Heart of a Waif* in 1915, and that was about the size of it. Since then a homonym called Claire Luce has created some confusion, and such is Clare's versatility that a ballplayer called Clair Luce would probably cause confusion too. But she is adamant that she cannot act at all when she is trying. Years later Congresswoman Luce starred briefly in a version of *Candida* in Stamford, as if to prove it. (The reviews were gleefully savage, as if the critics had been waiting for years.)

When people who excel at most things are only so-so at one of them, they're likely to exaggerate how badly they do it. So we'll never know for sure the quality of young Clare's acting. Either way, though, acting is at the core of things, as it has had to be with many successful women. Everything about her childhood sounds like the life of a star, certainly not of a politician or ambassador, and she has intimated that she always wanted to live like an actress without being one. So instead of comparing her with a pillar of the Republic like Eleanor Roosevelt, who didn't have to act her way to the top, one might try a Dietrich or Tallulah and imagine them transported into public life with all their mannerisms and scene-stealing tricks intact. At the very least, one might think of Eva Perón. Clare seems quite a sobersides by contrast.

Unfortunately, while Ann Snyder seemed hell-bent on nurturing a stage brat, Clare wanted, by the age of ten at least, to be something more like an intellectual—a category her mother could barely have heard of (surely it wasn't part of the American Dream?). So Clare's schooling was dangerously skimpy for someone of her intelligence. Three years of upper-middle-class gentility at St. Mary's in Garden City and Castle School in Tarrytown were her total schooling, plus some scraps of the public variety. That abbreviated education still seems to prey on Clare's mind as much as anything else in her whole life. "Just think of it: eight or nine honorary degrees, and I never finished high school," she says in a Mortimer Snerd voice. But this is looking on the bright side, and suggesting that everything turned out for the best. More often, she is not at all so sure. Education is the one variable, the unknown that could have affected the way she did everything later, could have changed her very style. It is maddening not to know.

She became instead the slightly stagy autodidact at the dinner table, reading everything she could lay hands on, Shaw, Nietzsche, Spengler, etc., but never sure she wasn't missing the one little clue, the scrap of intellectual etiquette, the corner of handkerchief that marks one as truly educated. In his life of Somerset Maugham, Ted Morgan reports a letter young Clare wrote to the Old Party bemoaning her unhappy childhood, announcing her plan to become a writer, and bemoaning again her mother's lack of sympathy for this plan.

Maugham's six-page answer is more a story about Maugham than about Clare. What is significant in light of Clare's 1949 recollections is that it tempers her sporadic claims to a happy childhood (other times she remembers the pain more vividly than the laughs). Every childhood is, no doubt, infinitely happy *and* unhappy. But the education question must have rankled sorely. Her mother no doubt loved Clare to distraction and was gallantly dedicated to making her a great lady, but she knew very well that intellect had nothing to do with this. Quite the reverse. Three years of schooling were more than enough for a great lady: after that one might become shrill and opinionated.

The schools Clare did pass through have the ring of social finishing schools to me, but perhaps that's just a general sense of female education as such in the 1910s. At any rate, Clare learned immeasurably more on her own than in these faded establishments. "She was always boss," says a schoolmate, by now fondly. "She always knew what she wanted." On the other hand, her early classmates called her "angel face." So the elements were already in place.

A yearbook is an unresponsive source, flashing the same blank smile on everyone. "Yes, yes, she is our prodigy and our genius," trills the Castle School "Drawbridge" of Ann Clare Boothe (that order), "yet just the same, she is as lovable as she is brilliant." It goes on to say that this paragon could do absolutely anything she tried: write, paint, and "you all know her wit." She would, it predicts, become famous someday as an author and illustrator.

Slightly more revealing is the section called "Who's Who," where the girls go up against each other. Clare is voted prettiest (which, if one can judge from a picture of the hockey team, must be the easiest prize she ever won), also the cleverest (though not the wittiest) and the most artistic. The things she didn't win are interesting too: she was not considered the most stylish, ambitious, graceful, or attractive, or even the best conversationalist—one wonders what happened to those who were. But she presumably got what she wanted, which right then was to be recognized as the class aesthete.

Years later, a *Life* cover story that never ran discovered all kinds of literary portents in the school years, prodigies of precocious writing; but wherever the *Lifer* found these, it was not in the old yearbook, a forum as closed to literature as it is to honest opinion. There is one somewhat bosomy poem called "The New Era" (subtitled "On seeing Miss Mary Mason's statue"), which concludes:

> Who am I?—Freedom and world bliss,
> Religion purer and clearer
> Sweet peace risen from war's abyss
> The triumph of the New Era!

This, as we'll see, is a precocious statement of some rock-bottom beliefs. But, trapped as it is in the brocade straitjacket of 1919 schoolgirl metrics, it can hardly be called writing at all. There is a piece of more promising light verse in the manner of Lewis Carroll: "They told me you had told to her what I had told to him," etc., (Kids do better with humor, because it isn't taught: there is no "right" way to do it) and finally a short-story melodrama that is almost as bad as one I wrote myself at that age. It shows bags of vocabulary and vigor and ghastly traces of all the junk one has read so far. In ensemble, her contributions thrum with high spirits, sufficient intelligence and a kind of innocence that would be suspect in a sixteen-year-old today.

Another, more Byronic note is struck by one last keepsake of the period: a photo of her number two dream man (next to Bernard Shaw), the poet John Drinkwater, which she herself inscribed "yours, John" (nothing as forward as "love," of course). For good measure, she wrote out a poem of Elizabeth Barrett Browning's on the back. The sumptuous loneliness of this reminds one of young Scott Fitzgerald, whom I can easily see doing this kind of thing on a bitter moonless night. (Clare was just the right age for a Scott heroine.) *Weltschmerz* was then an almost essential part of a literary adolescence—which doesn't mean that the loneliness wasn't real, and wouldn't recur.

That leaves us with "prettiest" to account for. Clare *was* chubby, and got up as high as 160 pounds in her teens. But she was clearly never the ugly duckling she claims to have felt like (significant in terms of later seductiveness. The ugly duckling tries harder). The school vote should certainly have been reassuring on this point. But I would guess from the photos of the period that she didn't need it. She knew she looked good, whatever she thinks now that she thought then.

If Castle School was a bit of a finishing school it may have come in handy at that. It was quite a classy place for a kid who'd made screen tests in Fort Lee, and who in background and pedigree both was and wasn't classy—a Boothe from Columbus Avenue being something like a Biddle from Flatbush. Although she now lived in Greenwich, and was a fast study, it seems likely that there was still some Professor Higginsing to be done as her mother pushed her energetically from square to square in the great American game. After graduation, Ann Boothe turned again to her *other* idea (she only had two, as far as I can make out), which was to enroll her daughter in acting school.

The game was briefly interrupted when Clare abruptly left home at seventeen to take a job cutting flowers in a paper factory. "I had to get away," she says simply, like Dickens dismissing his blacking-factory period. I imagine a spell of eerie equilibrium and sweet acquiescence followed by an inner explosion. This would happen again more than once in her life: bursts of petulance, like willpower boiling over. Sometimes these were serious, sometimes comically trivial, like the two days she wouldn't talk to me at Ridgefield (what *had* I done?). That little show was probably meant to teach me a lesson of some obscure sort: but I now believe that occasionally when Clare is thwarted, something goes crazy in the engine room. Those mighty turbines must be hard to control. And there could be a streak of intermittent depressiveness akin to her brother's to add to the mixture.

Anyway the escape into paper flowers was, by its very nature, temporary: a breather. In the long run it wouldn't have just thwarted her mother, it would have thwarted *her*, and her precious life of the mind. (You're not supposed to *end up* as a flower girl.) And the same went for just about any escape open to her. Clare could hardly get into Harvard at this point, or make a good marriage by herself. So while she might have some reservations about her mother's methods, there weren't many other methods available for a young woman who'd contracted ambition.

The one career that was open to women, the most democratic of all careers in my belligerent opinion, was literature, and Clare plugged away mightily at that during this same period. Unfortunately, at seventeen, she was far from finding a form that suited her. She still wrote poetry, but by now so bursting with Message that you can barely hear the music. "Success, the badge of true nobility" is one ominous line. Then there's a poem about Woodrow Wilson that goes: "Well, you had not the steel strength in your soul, / it was too soft to realize the goal ... The dream as such, is still a splendid dream / it's for our shattered hopes in you we grieve ... In your strange lexicon temerity / spelt courage, and swords-words, reflect meant pause, and stubbornness became sincerity." Beyond scolding the old President, Clare is clearly making up a list of do's and don'ts for herself. In *her* lexicon, a sword is a sword to this day.

It wasn't all furrowed brows, though. There's a nice little verse to her brother called "A Wife should be." It goes in part: "A wife should be quiet but never should gloom, / a wife should keep cheerful the tone of a room, / a wife should be able to manage her house / without driving crazy her venerable spouse." It's a fair takeoff on the moral instruction inflicted on young gentle-women, but it presages the game-playing Clare, who could dash off doggerel at top speed, rather than the real writing Clare, who may just be buried somewhere down in the rhetoric of the Wilson poem. In either case, she was years away (as who but a monster is not at seventeen?) from being a professional writer. And she had to pass the time somehow. Meanwhile there was Mama scheming away, this time back to her *first* idea, which was travel!

So Clare rejoined forces with Mrs. Boothe, perhaps on more equal terms, and the Big Push was on. By this time Ann, Sr., had acquired her new husband, Dr. Austin, who, according to Clare, was "New England cold" without a kiss or a hug for her or David, but decent enough otherwise. More to the immediate point (Clare was getting a bit big for a hugging stepfather), he was also a surgeon, who'd been given a grant to visit Germany. It wasn't enough to wave at the aristocracy when one got there, but it was a start.

American mothers and daughters must have been clogging the gangplanks in 1919 to get at what was left of Europe. And penniless noblemen must have lined the docks waiting for them. In the musical comedy version, the transaction was simple: a fortune for a title. But Clare was at a disadvantage. She was only beautiful. Stephen Shadegg* reports a poignant encounter with a Guards officer who

---

* Stephen Shadegg, *Clare Boothe Luce: A Biography* (New York: Simon & Schuster, 1970).

tracked her all the way back to America, only to turn the cab around when he saw her humble house.

Clare recalls a gruesome shooting weekend with some nobleman or other, spent trudging the moors in long underwear (jaegers, as they were then called). No title in the world was worth a life of that. In general, her romantic forays in England all have this soggy feel about them. One chap, whom she described as otherwise highly eligible, had a habit of lunging at her and banging his teeth on hers. She has never encountered such teeth to this day. What's more, "*All* Englishmen squeak when they're angry. I think they get it from squeaking at their nannies."

Allowing for the cooling and ironizing on the years, it seems reasonable to guess that her mother was working a bit harder at matchmaking for the sake of matchmaking than Clare—who perhaps sensed it wasn't going to be as difficult for her as it had been for Ann. Sometime around 1920, when they were back in America, the indefatigable mama swept Clare down to Hot Springs, Virginia, where the Prince of Wales was staying, because she was sure (as Clare recalls it) that the Prince was ripe for the taking, and would even give up his throne if he had to—proof that Mother studied these matters like racing forms.

The story is a fair guide to Mother's methods—and also to why they didn't invariably succeed. "My mother knew the manager of the Hot Springs Hotel. Mother's friends were odd characters like that. People who owned a department store or ran a hotel or something of the sort." The manager proceeded to arrange an actual ball, at which Clare would catch her Prince by the eye, and waltz him away from his boring old throne-to-come. All she had to do was upstage the year's slickest debutantes, led by (Clare isn't sure about this) one or more Vanderbilts, and backed, one assumes, by equally ruthless mothers, with infinitely larger bankrolls.

Unfortunately, Clare's luggage didn't show up and she had nothing to wear that night. Ann thrashed around Hot Springs all afternoon, but came up empty—a very fallible fairy godmother, fairly sobbing with vexation. So they spent the evening in their room, with Mother moaning to beat the band. A last forlorn effort was made the next day to catch the Prince's fishy eye with Clare's form off the diving board. But since she couldn't afford golfing clothes she never got within a mile of him—his loss, in her amused opinion today, considering the alternative. ("A sad little man," she concludes.)

Whether the blushful futility of such campaigns began to get to her, or whether an innate wish for something else began to assert itself, Clare soon ceased climbing, or being pushed, after wimpy little princes or teeth-clanging lesser title holders and began to edge toward her ultimate grail, self-made Americans. She seems to have had in the back of her mind a lofty, quasi-Shavian view of one's sexual vocation, as a mating of champions. The theater that influenced them both had improved since her mother's day and Clare was an ardent Shavian. But this instinct was hard to satisfy or even define, in the limited world her mother steered her through.

Clare in her innocence was still willing to believe that the intellectual company she craved could be found in the upper classes, although that trip to England turned up no evidence. The only small coup Mama brought off on that particular raid was an adroit movement of deck chairs during the voyage home, which placed Clare in the vicinity of Mrs. August Belmont: not only a good name to know, but a feminist who nudged Clare a little in that significant direction. Mrs. Belmont was referred to at various times as the Lenin or Mussolini of the embryonic movement, and actually wanted to start an all-women political party. Clare later dropped some leaflets for Mrs. Belmont over Syracuse, New York, which may, who knows, have borne fruit.

With such shaky entrees into Society, Mrs. Austin and daughter settled in Old Greenwich, Connecticut, to await, or encourage, developments. Developments turned out to be one George Brokaw, the charming, tipsy heir to a garment business fortune. The Belmont maneuver had finally paid off. (If you had to move your deck chair next to only one person, you could hardly have done better than this well-connected idealist.) As Clare tells it, the marriage, 1923, was arranged practically behind her back, like a baseball trade—Mother's last deal; but this did not keep the Brokaw relatives from whispering the word "prostitute" in her hearing ("Actually, I was the most timid of virgins"). No one seems able to remember any reason at all for marrying Brokaw *except* his money, but Clare says he was nice enough when sober (she didn't know about his drinking then) and he did manage to sire a bright, attractive daughter, Ann—the only child Clare was to have, though she says she always wanted more, and tried more than once. (She was to have at least three miscarriages over the years, and she once tried half-heartedly to abort herself with hot baths, etc., because she thought a baby would upset Brokaw just then. This method seemed, if anything, to produce healthier, spunkier infants and it apparently didn't prevent Ann, after which it didn't matter. An operation in the late 1930s showed that one was her limit anyway.)

In a fit of grandiosity, Brokaw decided to transfer his summer drinking from Piping Rock, Long Island, to a Vanderbilt pile named Beach Mound in Newport, Rhode Island. This brought Clare bang up against the Wimbledon, the Grand Prix, the very Olympics of snobbery. Newport easily rebuffed the cream of the new Irish society, the Murrays, Cuddihys, and MacDonells—driving them all the way to Southampton (where they could rebuff the Kellys and Kennedys), so one can imagine the ice on the verandas as the upwardly-striving Clare Boothe Brokaw hove into sight.

Even openly ambitious men were frowned on in these circles: ambitious women were monsters. Clare pluckily gave Sunday afternoon musicales, to which nobody came (according to a letter writer, who probably meant the term in its technical sense, as in "Nobody was in New York last week,") either because one simply didn't play music on a polo day, or one didn't play *that* music. My informant says she felt very touched by young Clare, sitting brave and alone at these and other gatherings and being snubbed by the world's finest. But she needn't have worried. Clare was already storing up spitballs which would appear a year or so after she divorced Brokaw in *Stuffed Shirts* and settle these scores once and for all. This collection of stories would be Clare's statement about Society, the magic mountain women like her had to climb if they wanted to climb at all in the twenties: a mountain composed of diamonds and quicksand.

Her chosen angle of vision shows up in the very first piece, "Where the Blue Blood Begins." A floundering outsider from New Rochelle commits a gaffe in the presence of one Mrs. Towerly, the lead battleship of New York Society, and Mrs. Towerly guns her down for it. The powder room attendant is observed (by the author) to smile sympathetically: but at which of the two women "is a matter for conjecture."

In later stories, it is not always quite clear whom Clare is smiling at, either. Mrs. "old family" Towerly wins a few and loses a few. She is clearly better than her rival, Mrs. "upstart" Topping, because her victories are effortless (the names are rather heavily ironic, as in Emily Post's Book of Etiquette—which I found, thickly underlined, in Clare's Honolulu library in 1977). Mrs. Towerly is at least the right stuff, and the author seems alternately to sneer at and rather admire her regal put-downs, as if she herself were alternately sneering at and admiring the creamy, dripping decor of the super-rich. This ambivalence about the world her mother half got her into remains to this day. And if she seems now occasionally a bit of a Mrs. Towerly, she is also the smiling attendant.

When it appeared in 1930, *Stuffed Shirts* would set off some satisfactory yelps from Society, proving that it had scored a hit. There was a clamor of claimers and disclaimers of identity, as there would be later with *The Women:* Truman Capote couldn't have asked for anything more. A small reputation as a grateless wretch was launched.

Her own recollection of the Brokaw-Newport period (c. '23–'29) emphasizes a more poignant and Clare-like aspect of social unease. Since her new neighbors were virtually all Hasty Puddings who'd been tapped for Bones, or whatever one does at Ivy League colleges, she assumed that they must be educated people. So she launched into solemn intellectual discussions with them, volleying her Spengler and Nietzsche into the crowd and receiving no return fire whatever. In the crushing silence of a Newport night, she figured she must be doing something wrong. These people were being clever behind her back—that was it. With only those three years of schooling, she had learned a great many words by sight that she had never actually heard spoken. So she lived in dread of mispronunciation and misuse, not to mention the larger misunderstandings.

Little did she realize that most of her auditors would not have known the difference. So far were they from having read her beloved Shaw and Spengler, these people could almost be called functional illiterates. Her grim and lifelong battle to establish intellectual credentials began with some of the dimmest men ever to splice a mainbrace.

It's interesting that my Newport correspondent ever found her touching, though, because nobody would believe this now. Clare's infuriating poise had obviously not been perfected yet, and certain insecurities peeped out, even while she toughed it out in her lonely salon. Perhaps this helps to explain how someone as willful as Clare could have stood still for an arranged marriage with a dodo. Outside of that, Clare's degree of assent to the Brokaw years can only be guessed at. Despite the rubric of the day whereby parents circled like mastodons to win an edge for their passive young, a clever daughter could sometimes steer her mastodon in a desired direction. And Clare had been good at getting her way even in grammar school.

A history of the mother/daughter combines that climbed their way in tandem through the twenties calls for a Jane Austen, or at

least a Nancy Mitford. Clare's mad dash for the paper company in
her teens was the only open rift, but surely two such willful women
must have fought more than once. Social advancement calls for a
thousand tactical decisions, and the author of *Stuffed Shirts* had to
feel she was better at these than her grizzled veteran of a mother,
who was the equivalent of last war's generals. At the same time, I
guess from her conversation that Clare felt compassion for this gal-
lant, slightly comic creature who had battled so long to keep them
afloat. (Mrs. Austin, we can take it, was the woman from New Rochelle who made the gaffe in *Stuffed Shirts*. Clare had to be stoical for
two.) And again how many choices were there, besides being a
prize pony or pumpkin? It wasn't exactly a new fate for women, or
one that took them unawares. What society overlooked, as it began
to glare venomously at Clare, was that *she* was the catch by any rational standard, and that old George Brokaw was lucky to have her.
Who remembers him now?

Anyway, Clare is adamant that it was her mother's decision,
not hers, and I believe she's right, because of the way she tells it.
Clare has several kinds of anecdote, in some of which she sounds
passive, as in "Harry persuaded me to do this, Bernie said why
don't you do that," as if she'd never had a thought in her pretty
head; and in others of which it is she who is telling Harry, "Why
don't you start a magazine?" or, "Franklin, why don't we give them
a New Deal?" She likes these stories, which run great events to
earth in offhand conversations in forgotten living rooms: either
way, guileless or visionary, she becomes a conduit of magic, which
is a very old-fashioned way of being a woman.

The point about Brokaw is that he is not an anecdote. He just
happened. Her marriage to him is not a cute story, and she doesn't
try to make it so, any more than she does with her mother, brother,
or any hard reality: although once the brute facts of Brokaw are
disposed of, there are about two and a half laughs left over, to cover
a six-year marriage. Brokaw indeed proved, between bouts of in-
sipidity, to be an ugly, murderously violent drunk, whose only
contribution to human betterment was his trick of hiding gin in his
golf trophies. On the road to delirium, he occasionally passed
through a valley of despond where he talked about how he should
have been a Presbyterian missionary (both Clare's husbands had
this curious tendency). He even attempted sometimes to play the
stirring phrase "The good, the true and the beautiful" on the banjo,
with predictably strange results.

Funny now, but a nightmare then. All Clare's dreams of being a great writer, or anything else, dribbled away bit by bit. Her year-book yearnings joined the other hot air in that volume. Brokaw didn't go to work, although he did occasionally go to golf, and it was impossible to get down to anything ambitious in his gloomy presence. Because when sober he was sodden with remorse, and when drunk he just tootled along until his faithful manservant came rolling up with the straitjacket. Literally, says Clare. In between, he swatted Clare around enough, possibly, to have produced those miscarriages: the school of hard knocks indeed, long before Clare entered public life.

Clare had no one to confide in about any of this except her mother ("With a father it might have been entirely different"). It speaks for the solitude of her school years that she had "no contemporary friends, no home to go to." Ann Austin moved in with the Brokaws and professed to find the situation not so very terrible: she was used to getting her own lumps in life, and pricing them exactly. She advised Clare just to hang in there gamely until George drank himself to death—not such a long wait, it seemed. Clare recoiled from this ghoulish counsel. She wanted out right now, on any terms. She tried living in the Stanhope Hotel for a short while, but finally gave up and headed for Reno in 1929, with a contrite George Brokaw practically hanging from the train asking for another chance.

Clare got her divorce—and the germ of a scene for *The Women*. She accepted what she considers a modest settlement from George, guaranteeing her $26,000 a year for life, and a nice little trust fund, a small nick off a large fortune. Modesty is always comparative anyhow, and perhaps she could have shaken him down for more—he was not obsessively faithful—but she couldn't wait to find out ("I may have married for money but I certainly didn't divorce for it"). Brokaw's next wife had George committed to a home almost immediately and soon after collected a real bundle. This was the future wife of Henry Fonda, who later killed herself, and—who knows—some of the money may have wound its way down to help support a Jane Fonda peace initiative. It's a perfect Clare story. Fortunes often bound around in these O. Henry ways, and you just have to be a good sport about it.*

* According to Howard Teichmann's book *Mr. Fonda* (NAL Publishers, N.Y., Nov. 1981), Frances Brokaw Fonda also earned everything she got. Brokaw beat her up as he had Clare, prior to drowning mysteriously in the sanitarium swimming pool. Frances also confirmed the story of Clare's miscarriages.

Anyway, Clare was in a pleasant position in 1929 at the age of twenty-six and has been in one ever since: not quite super-rich, which would have been a burden—all her careers would be suspect—but always rich enough to experiment. The marriage to Brokaw was her first and hardest career and it made the others possible, or at least easier. Unfortunately, it also built a glass wall between her and the depression and was a latent cause of resentment. The columnist Mark Sullivan's daughter, Sydney Walling, remembers that "Clare had quantities of money. She had a beautiful apartment at River House—a huge, square white living room which you entered through a door in a long wall of books. On her door was a wooden clock face and she set the hands to the time when she wanted the maid to bring her breakfast. When she left the house, one maid would help her into her magnificent fur coat and another would spray her with perfume from a big atomizer. Very different from the home life of the dear Queen."

Nevertheless "she *wanted* to be a queen," says her old friend Arlene Francis, "and why the hell not?" Clare had now reached the outer limits of her mother's dream: Ann Snyder had seen no further, except perhaps to see more of same—bigger millionaires, better polo ponies. For a while Clare lived it out loyally and to the hilt (how am I doing, Ma?). She was whispered to have a social advisor, not so uncommon in those days, but good for a giggle perhaps. Rumor also had our gay divorcee being dressed by four maids at once—and rumor was as good as reality for a queen, as she later underlined by having flowers sent to herself (by rumor again) at her office, when she had an office. Flowers, dressing room—these are actress stories. Every time Clare left the house she was mounting a stage.

This was the swashbuckling Clare of the late twenties, who seemed to be entering the Jazz Age just as everyone else was leaving. There is no point pretending she wasn't enjoying every last soap bubble—it was her dream too, up to a point, and would always be. But curiously, these years also rate high on her silence meter; because part of her is disgusted by them. Immediately after her breakup with Brokaw, she says she underwent a spasm of finding wealth and success repulsive, as one might find snakes and insects—presumably a reaction to early force-feeding. And even after making her rather spectacular peace with the good life she still felt there was something second-rate about it. "I wish I had gone to Europe instead," she says now. New York was trashy, vulgar, and seductive and she made the most of it. But she feels that there must have been better ways to do the elusive thing—be a Superior Woman—than she could see from Manhattan. "If only I had had someone to talk to," she says. (In the Summer of '49, she asked me once whom I would turn to if I needed serious advice, and I answered without thinking, "My father, I guess." The answer seemed to astound and delight her, and she repeated it to others a couple of times more than I thought it was worth. Only now do I understand why she did so.)

As it was, armed with her Shaw and her Spengler, she had to figure it all out for herself—how to be an intellectual and a queen, in a country unfavorable to both. The last few years with Brokaw and the first months after constitute one of her times in the desert, years spent trying to determine who she was and what she was for. She drifted aimlessly for a while, even in and out of a psychiatrist's office at record speed, with no role in sight, let alone the four or five that were about to spring at her. Destiny, of course, always seems inevitable afterwards. But at the time there was no reason to suppose that Clare would ever be famous for anything except the size of her atomizer. Back in 1929, Clare had no career models, no counselors worth a damn, nothing but her own mother wit. She simply had to invent herself, for better or worse.

To get down to practicalities: there was clearly no future for her in the Brokaw world. The family still despised her as a fortune hunter, and families like that know how to make these things clear, having a lot of time to devote to it. She must already have been bored stiff anyway. A posh life trying on dresses was only supportable if you were Someone trying on dresses: one would need a hush and a whisper of salesgirls and a scraping of managers, to enjoy that particular dream.

Clare had her own daughter Ann now, whom she loved ardently if fitfully, and at times she felt that that was enough—though she was determined not to replay Mrs. Boothe's role of professional mother. Ann had the most normal upbringing that money could buy.

The years with Ann were kept obstinately private, and most of Ann's letters to Clare are out of bounds not only to me, but to Clare herself in that dreaded box in Honolulu, which I can't help thinking of as a partly melodramatic development. If Ann wrote anything especially painful, Clare wouldn't have to look it up. Such outside sources as Clare's "favorite niece" (on the Luce side) Libby Warner assure me that Ann and her mother were very warm and natural together; in fact, the phrase that pops up more than once is that Ann "adored her mother." Of course, she had to do some of her adoring at a distance when Clare later hit the road to lecture or report. But Clare was always ingenious at budgeting her time. I'm amazed at how many photos even in her busiest years show her relaxing. And the ones taken with Ann suggest that the two of them were too *comfortable* together to be strangers.

But just bringing up her daughter was not a career. Clare had just not been fashioned to be either a homebody or a jewel horse. For a while she seems to have been known as a socialite at large, and I'm sure she did it with sparkle, because that's the way you do it (she is a stickler for technique). But after years of this with Brokaw and months of spinning her wheels without him, she decided that if other vocations would not call her, she would call them. So she got herself a job.

Careers were a comparatively new mountain for women, and in no time Clare was accused of climbing it the old way, charming her way ever upwards. It would have been difficult not to, considering her alleged power to drop men to their knees. For instance, her managing editor of *Vanity Fair*, Donald Freeman, fell openly and hopelessly in love with her, though no one has claimed that she used this, because by good chance Frank Crowninshield called the tunes, not Freeman.

The whole story is an early example of a no-win Clare situation: short of having her good looks removed by surgery, there was no way of proving she'd done *anything* without their assistance. Femininity could not be neutral: it either helped you or crippled you. Clare presumably took no chances on the latter, although the few affairs I heard rumored most often were with men in no special position to help. But the point is that Clare was also pretty good at what she did, starting with that very first job.

It has often been told (by herself as it happens) how (in 1929) she sat in the Condé Nast offices, unhired and unwanted, writing picture captions for *Vogue*, which *Vogue* vaguely ran without knowing who she was. This is the kind of story that's pleasant if you like the protagonist, but with a very slight tilt becomes part of the conniving Clare legend: rich woman angles for job she doesn't need. But in fact the rich woman *had* to angle in this case, because she was at a curious disadvantage. Condé Nast had expressly told Clare at some dinner or other that he would never hire her because Society ladies had no stamina. (He later may have changed his mind about this because Society ladies also make no demands.) So Clare barged into the office, learned that one of the caption writers was missing, and announced brightly that that's exactly what she was sent for. I think Clare likes the story because she would rather be thought Machiavellian than a vamp, doing what she called "monkey jobs," which involve hanging by one's tail. Anyway, none of this would matter with anyone else, because she wrote perfectly good captions.

She had to, to hold her first real job (a year later), which was on *Vanity Fair*, *Vogue*'s bright-sister publication in the Nast chain. Although it ran the best text a smallish budget could buy (i.e., throwaway pieces by famous writers, brighter ones by unknowns, and a barrel of staff-written filler, published under a panoply of pen names), *Vanity Fair* really lived on its photographs, particularly its portrait photographs, which cried out for captions, cheeky or sonorous, as the case might be. (Dorothy Parker had worked there, setting a very fast pace for wit. "Brevity is the soul of lingerie" first appeared in *V.F.*) And the magazine was much too small to carry a dumb blonde. Besides, its editor in chief, Frank Crowninshield, was too cool and elusive a creature to do anything so self-destructive. Packing the place with pretty secretaries was enough of that sort of thing.

"You have a young man under your bed," said Crowninshield when he saw the captions. "That was the first taste," she says, "of always having a man under your bed before you did anything." Naturally it was the first taste—it was only her first job.

"Crownie" has always sounded like a twenties cartoon to me, the dandy who keeps things light, the guy who tells you a mildly improper joke when your heart is breaking and makes it all right: but whose own heart is never breaking. Edmund Wilson, an earlier employee, described him distastefully in his memoir of the twenties. "With a gait at once strutting and mincing . . . The born courtier who lacks an appropriate court." Crowninshield also taught Wilson to distrust the word "gentleman" ever after. Wilson adds that men who worked for Crownie, such as Robert Benchley, did not care for him, but that he was great at charming those secretaries.

Edmund Wilson had a low tolerance for fops (he couldn't even see the point of P. G. Wodehouse), and here he makes the worst case for one: the smallness and slight moral seediness of it all. Yet for the wandering souls of the twenties, like Clare and her sidekick Helen Brown Norden (later Lawrenson), Crownie was a reassuring figure, a cork bobbing safely on the Manhattan turbulence, and they both loved him like an uncle. He may also have passed on

some of his own lightness and urbanity to what, if her poetry's anything to go on, might have become a somewhat heavy-handed style.
Because in no time Clare was writing some pretty funny pieces for
him, parodies and make-believe conversations (Gandhi meets
Garbo kind of thing) under the name Jerome Jerome and others, as
well as captions for her own mordantly named department "we
nominate for oblivion." Great finger exercises for anyone. Once
again, as if to establish her credentials for all time, Clare submitted
her first piece under a pen name. Only when it was accepted did
she come out in the open.

But the aspect of the magazine she talked about most (and I
listened to least, alas) during that Summer of mine was not writing
but photography, particularly the work of the maestros, Stieglitz
and Steichen. I remember imagining, as I skimmed through Clare's
bound volumes, a lobby jammed with celebrities, jostling to have
their pictures taken. *Vanity Fair* must have practically met the boats
and brought the first-class list over in steam cars. Nobody left town
without his mug shots recorded.

Thus began Clare's professional association with Celebrity as
such. And if she threw herself into it with indecent abandon, as old
friend Helen Norden Lawrenson darkly suggests, by waylaying and
entrapping social lions, she was just doing her job (call it a silly job
if you like—but Norden met a lot of famous people too, and wrote
about them later with profit). It was certainly a felicitously chosen
career to advance in, because doing it well almost demanded self-
promotion. And no doubt Clare pursued her targets, her little
Churchills and Maughams, with fiendish ingenuity, in the best *Front
Page* tradition—though there is no record of her dressing up as a
plumber or meter reader as others in her trade have done—using
her good looks to the full (imagine a *Front Page* reporter with such
looks *not* using them); but the magazine did need the pictures and
stories the victim provided, and she landed enough of them to be
made managing editor in 1933: a professional acknowledgment
and not a beauty contest prize. (She also learned an ear-bending lot
about photography.)

Something else she used besides her looks was her late-Empire
style, faintly operatic, left over from the previous reign when she
had to joust with real-life Towerlys and Toppings. I like to picture a
dowager here in full regalia, pounding the block—diverting, and I
wouldn't put it past her. But I'm afraid she only looked like that to
the ink-stained wretches of the press. Photographs suggest that she
owned the world's greatest supply of business suits and dresses.

Unfortunately one can't smell them to find out if she was staggering under the load of perfume that usually rounds off these accounts.

But really I think the subject is aura: a personal manner as alien to a pressroom, that seedy redoubt of democracy, as Harry Luce's. (Since *Vanity Fair* was not your ordinary pressroom, she may have received some furtive competition in the dressing-up department.) A friend of mine who studies these things advises me that successful career women tend to spring from strong fathers, so tend to act somewhat masculine; Clare did not even have a strong mother in that sense, but a cannily feminine one, which, even today, is probably considered a bizarre style in management circles.

It is hard to believe from the regal accounts of her that she was just thirty when she got the job, and not some battle-hardened veteran of Café Society. She was feeling her way—but arrogantly. Don't let them know you're frightened. One person who was impressed by this performance, while apparently seeing through it (he called her "the poor kid") was the next significant man in her life: Bernard Baruch, Society's favorite sage, whom she met on her *Vanity Fair* rounds.

Baruch was a self-made legend, and there was a lot to be learned from one of those. "Advisor to Presidents" he was called, a modest enough title when you consider the competition over the years. But what really distinguished him was his second title, "the man on the park bench." This took genius. While still fresh from his day's advising at the White House or wherever, Baruch would hold court from a bench in Lafayette Park to anyone who asked him. This was not only plumb in the lovable, no-airs American tradition, but it allowed him to embroider his own role a touch here and a touch there until at times he seemed the sole architect of everything good in the American economy. The mere clatter of dropped names ("As I said to Woodrow") was enough to do it.

Uniquely, Baruch managed to maintain a man-behind-the-scenes image throughout all this. Open to the public, yet privy to the President's ear, he must have been the first out-front *éminence grise* in history. As Dorothy Parker once said, there were two things she could never figure out: the theory of the zipper, and the precise function of Bernard Baruch. Yet everything about him told you he must have one, probably a mighty important one: he had what the French call *l'art de se faire valoir* (the knack of writing your own price tag) to as high a degree as Clare was ever accused of; and precisely because he was willing to remain always a consort, never a battleship, he became a great one, a star in his own right—and a wonderful model for a woman.

Not that Clare set out to study him; she simply, insofar as one can apply the word from this distance, fell for him. It was not a strain: he was a striking-looking man, one of the few celebrities, according to the otherwise disrespectful J. K. Galbraith, whose real-life appearance did not let you down one bit. Tall, craggy, white-haired, all that kind of thing (Clare once told me that her physical "type" was Lee Marvin, the horse-faced one), Baruch, like Harry Luce later, was a catch even if he'd never made a dime. As to his vaunted intelligence, while nothing could have lived up to the Olympian press releases, it was quite good enough to satisfy Clare's love affair with brains. It was, oddly, for a man who talked so much, a laconic, quasi-rustic intelligence. Although Baruch had made millions in mining and speculation backing his own mysterious judgment, when I asked Clare quick quick for a phrase to remember him by, "Work and save" was the first thing she could come up with. A Vermont farmer could have said no less.

When Baruch was very old, he told Clare, "I can still be intelligent but I don't feel like it," and that I consider a bright remark. But otherwise he is not remembered for anything he said, even in his autobiography,* which is a seamlessly banal and disingenuous work. But Clare hardly needed to learn verbal facility from him. Baruch was shrewd and tough, a living example of self-made self-reliance, heady confirmation of the things Clare's mother taught her. A father who did what a father was supposed to do, unlike her own.

Baruch couldn't marry Clare or anyone else, because of a mentally troubled wife at home. (He kept telling her to wait—but his wife didn't die until six months after Clare married Harry Luce.) Her interest in Baruch suggests that there would be no more Brokaws in her life. The frontal assault on Society was over; she had done what her mother wanted. Now the subject was politics. If you hung out with the advisor to Presidents, you had to expect some advice yourself. And for the first time, Clare learned how the world was run and paid for from a Baruch point of view.

Baruch was a fiscal conservative but a lifelong Democrat (these terms were not as contradictory then as they became). And two of Clare's first political articles for *Vanity Fair* in the very early thirties

---

* *Baruch: My Own Story* (New York: Holt, 1957).

were about New York's jolliest Democrats, Al Smith and Jimmy Walker.

These articles are interesting specimens in the evolution of journalism, because they provide practically no information whatever, certainly none you would need to leave the office to get. They depend entirely on flourishes of wit and style. For instance, the piece on Smith starts with a lyric evocation of New York's Lower East Side that could be applied to almost any essay on anything, like those old movie openings of bustling streets. At no point is it made clear whether the author has actually met Smith (though she had), or what he was like up close. The essayist wings it on virtuosity and press clippings: not a report but a performance.

Turning to the straight political pieces Clare began to bring into *Vanity Fair* as editor, one finds a yet further remove of abstraction. Walter Lippmann did some of them, and even his are all what are known in the trade as "thumbsuckers"; i.e., the reader learns nothing from them that he didn't know already, except possibly what a beautiful mind the writer has. A dateline would have been pointless. The same piece could have been written in Washington or Pago Pago, this year or last. If Lippmann had any inside information, he obviously thought it unsporting to use it in *Vanity Fair* (as we know, he used it like mad elsewhere). Instead, we get pure cerebration, which modern readers may undervalue. It was tough enough for Clare to get the frivolous Crowninshield, let alone Condé Nast, the tsar of all the *Vogues*, to share her new political interests, without heaping a lot of facts on them as well. So the pieces had to justify themselves first and last as entertainment.

Clare herself still writes a bit in this tradition. Whether she's taking on defense spending or abortion, you will get precious few facts, except maybe one or two calculated to startle. Otherwise, everything hangs on the originality of her ideas, a terrible burden for a writer to inflict on herself. The effect nowadays is to make the writer seem rather opinionated—but that is precisely what one was paid to be in the old days. Clare remains sturdily a magazine essayist of the thirties, no more or less opinionated than Lippmann, or Jay Franklin, who packed the most fevered political brain at *Vanity Fair*.

Jay Franklin, or his ideas, influenced the next bend in Clare's career. He believed that America needed a new political party, for which he proposed the vaguest platform in the rich history of vague platforms. Armed with this, and a name—"the New National party"—and a few friends, he marched on Chicago for the Democratic Convention of 1932, with Clare tagging along as window dressing with Bernard Baruch. She took the opportunity to float a notion—borrowed from Mrs. Belmont, facetiously or otherwise—of making Franklin's brainchild a women-led party (Lippmann said "I'll join"), and one of the gang, she forgets which, did indeed coin the phrase "New Deal," thinking little of it. Except for its staying power, it is not much of a phrase.

Once there, their abstractness caught up with them fast. They had no delegates, and didn't know where to find them, and they had no leverage at all. It is hard to imagine sophisticated New Yorkers knowing so little about how politics works, and one can only conclude that they'd been reading each other's stuff. Roosevelt was amused to have them around as a buffer between him and serious opposition, but they weren't even up to that. Within a day they had not so much capitulated as evaporated, and gone over to Roosevelt or gone home. Such was their evanescence that I was unable to find a single reference to them in the Chicago press of the day. A party that exists only in its own mind is of course quite in the American grain.

Clare was twenty-nine and politically inexperienced even in this crowd. She would never make the mistake again. She might still write abstractly, but she began to learn the nuts and bolts of the master, Franklin D. Roosevelt himself, to whom Baruch routinely introduced her, before unloading his latest advice. Later, FDR's hearty-male condescension to Clare would have unwanted consequences, and he may have regretted getting her started in even a humble way, because after campaigning vigorously against the Republicans, she became in her terms, the scullery maid in Roosevelt's kitchen cabinet, close enough to the stove to see the New Deal being prepared. (Her specific niche was in a wing of the NRA called the Theater Code Board, and all she remembers about it is that you can't get theater people to agree to anything.)

People are still surprised to hear of what sounds like a left-wing lapse in such a conservative life. But Clare wasn't actually born conservative, and she was to lapse much further a little later in the thirties when Harry Bridges had her briefly in two minds about the Communist party. Working for FDR was no such clear ideological choice. "Make no mistake, it was fascism," she says of the first one hundred days of the New Deal; and indeed Italy was the parallel that came to critics' minds more often than Russia.*

The hot question of the thirties was whether capitalism could survive at all without force. Roosevelt made the force appear to come from the people, but then so did Mussolini at first. Central organization always makes a country work better for a while, and every Tom, Dick, and Harry thinks *he's* the one who's doing it.

Like many a New Dealer turned conservative, Clare now says that the party left her, not vice versa. And if we allow for her interpretation of what she saw in Washington, this is not as far-fetched in her case as it usually is. As a congresswoman, she would be constrained, if only by her constituency, to take several liberal positions. But even now, in her conservative retirement, she believes that government should step in smartly to help the needy. During one of our recent unemployment blights, she came out for government work projects, obviously patterned on the New Deal. And more recently, she was pleased to tell me that New York's financial crisis was *not* caused by welfare recipients. The powder room attendant lives on, inside Mrs. Towerly if necessary, and Clare's domestic policy always has been much gentler than her big-stick foreign policy.

Anyway, prior to Luce, Clare was not considered primarily political by anyone but herself. (If she had trouble being taken seriously as a writer of captions, you can imagine her chances as a political theorist.) She had, as editor of *Vanity Fair* in its last years of existence, politicized that flossy paper quite a bit; but 1929 might have done that anyway. The smart chat of the twenties became harder to sell, or to believe in, after the Crash. But impressions of Clare at that time are anything but political. Irwin Shaw, the boy wonder writer from Brooklyn, talks of her and Helen Brown Norden as two glamorous kids about town, a formidable team before the rather one-sided hair-pulling began years later.† Shaw says they were both "brave as lions. They would go anywhere and talk to anybody. And they weren't afraid to experiment." He adds

---

* Current concepts of Left and Right should not be slapped casually onto the New Deal. To the Left of the day, it looked like the slipperiest of capitalist tricks to keep itself in business. And at least some capitalists saw how this might be so. For instance, the inevitable Baruch was to recommend *complete* wage and price controls in World War II—a use of big government that even a liberal like Galbraith gagged on. But business' true feelings about big government, then and now, are too delicate to concern us here. They certainly didn't concern Clare that much. Her ultimate calling would be foreign policy, and her most famous cry against Roosevelt would be that "he lied us into war."

† For more on Lawrenson, see Chapter Seven.

jokingly that there was nothing much to experiment with in those days except sex. But when I asked him specifically about Clare, he said, "She played the field but she never played me." Who was in the field and what was played there is very faded gossip—old-timers would have to strain to remember the alleged names—and anyhow seems secondary to the performance itself. Striding into a speakeasy and accosting a gangster was much harder for a woman to do than sleeping around. And Clare's reputation was being built on brashness, not promiscuity. One name that does survive the period is Buckminster Fuller, the sage with the geodesic dome, who claims, I'm told, that Clare married Luce on the rebound from him. Whether or not this is strictly true, it makes some sort of sense. Fuller is an intellectual adventurer, not a social butterfly and Clare always speaks fondly of "Bucky." Finally, he has a big head (literally) which is a common attribute of Clare's beaux.

This was Clare's swinging period, and she threw herself into it with her usual thoroughness. Either she or Lawrenson (I believe the latter) actually coined the phrase "Café Society," for that meritocracy of foppishness and social inutility which was gradually driving real Society* into the back pages, and which fit the phrase and the magazine *Vanity Fair* to perfection. Café Society's great spawning ground was Broadway, and Clare had all the contacts there that she could possibly need, before she even knew what to do with them.

It was inevitable that Clare would write plays—in fact, she started at the age of ten, and committed a couple of unproduced ones in the ensuing years—because dialogue is her very essence. *Vanity Fair* was always in an uproar of talk, and Jeanne Ballot, who worked there from the Edmund Wilson era on, tells me that while Clare was not memorably witty in the office, she was a marvelous take, very retentive and swift at passing around and embellishing the anecdotes that made up much of the conversation. For a managing editor she seems to have let the place lapse into locker room jocularity deplorably easily.

The icy Clare of legend has a special kind of goofy grin for of-

---

* *Stuffed Shirts,* written during and just after the Crash, kissed Society, as symbolized by Newport, good-bye. That tiny never-never land which began less than a hundred years earlier with Commodore Vanderbilt spitting on his carpets in lieu of a christening was not the stuff of pyramids. Society of the *real* old sort did survive the depression, but rather like the Hollywood studios in our era: the *real* money and power were all over the place now and Clare was nearer to both than the old families.

fice memories, and she wears it full force when she recalls, for instance, an article she'd edited herself that mysteriously had the good old Prince of Wales following Brenda Frazier, the ultimate debutante, into the bathroom instead of the ballroom—a piece of irredeemable childishness that casts a nice light on the slaphappy mood at the magazine ("I was a very good editor . . . and I'd read the article three times," she says with that oafish grin).

Miss Ballot confirms that Clare was a good editor, who worked hard at the drudgery: layouts, scheduling, and whatnot. It sounds like a well-rounded life, what with massages at the Waldorf and celebrity office lunches, for the likes of Thomas Wolfe and Aldous Huxley—at which *Clare* on occasion was known to hold forth.

Clare had formed a sensible habit of boning up on a man's specialty in advance, which her critics consider malevolent (presumably a journalist should keep her mind completely blank up to the last moment), but sometimes it became too much for her, and she forgot whose specialty they were talking about. This must have made her a bulldozer of a coquette: one who would rather be taken seriously than to bed any day, and who used every feminine wile just to get a hearing. But I believe it also harks back to her days as a society hostess when, sandwiched forever between two strange men (never women), you'd better have something to say, or go slowly mad with boredom. Anyway, if she was already collecting dialogue for the stage a generous amount of it was her own.

*Vanity Fair* could well have been voted the magazine least likely to survive the slump, although it made a fist of it. *Vanity Fair* was as expensive to produce as sister *Vogue*, without a mass audience to support it. It was not, at the other extreme, quite an elite magazine in the sense of a *Fortune* or *American Heritage*, which can raise prices until only your doctor can afford it. It was a street magazine like *Variety*, only classier. And that kind of product, offering vulgarity for the discerning, was a vanishing luxury, like the smoking jacket. So while much of the Broadway world was folding its tent anyway and creeping toward Hollywood, *Vanity Fair* quietly disappeared into (or was swallowed whole by) *Vogue* in 1936. But by then Clare had long since swum ashore with the plans for *Life* magazine in her teeth.

Although *Life* was still several years away, Clare's blueprint dates back to the *Vanity Fair* years ('30–'36). *Life* was about the best you could do in an age of mass production, if you wanted the best photography, as Clare did (writers you could get for nothing, as always, and *Esquire* became maybe the closest thing to *Vanity Fair* in that department for the remains of the decade). *Life* was to be a sort of *Vanity Fair* for the masses. It would still be spellbound by Names, but without the old, we-precious-few irony; it would be as handsome as ever, but in a streamlined, less idiosyncratic way. The satire—well, perhaps that's putting it too strongly. There's no point in dissecting, or lamenting, the differences here, because it wound up not being Clare's magazine after all. One of the men whom Clare had nominated for *Vanity Fair*'s Hall of Fame fetched up with both Clare and the magazine, one under each arm. Henry R. Luce was about to come "whut-whutting" into view (1935, to be precise), and we'll get to him in a moment. But already Clare was eyeing another career: following the arc of vocation that ran from the satirical exchanges of *Stuffed Shirts* through the imaginary dialogues (the *Pope* meets Garbo, etc.) of *Vanity Fair*, she began writing her own plays.

Because her playwriting was an extension of her *Vanity Fair* self, and not of Harry Luce, I've decided to hold him at bay a moment longer. Although Luce did in fact marry Clare toward the beginning of this career, and would perhaps have something to do with its termination, he had no discernible impact on the plays themselves—except perhaps as unwitting material. He did read bits aloud to her, and I've always wondered what parts he read in *The Women*, but his attitude at first seems to have been one of goofy admiration. The mighty professional team of Clare and Harry had not been forged yet, so it's important to keep them separate while we can, to show how much of Clare's career was actually Clare's.

She wrote, like most young playwrights, several plays that weren't produced, but since the analysis of unproduced plays has never really caught on, I've decided to skip them, along with the misbegotten *Abide with Me*,* which unfortunately was produced, and stick to her three successes. A Broadway play is so much an event, designed down to the bit parts to explode in your face on one particular night, that it is hard to judge any one of them fairly from the scrawny instructions known as a script. In late 1936 *The Women* certainly exploded, to a splutter of critics, and has done so ever since in many productions in the most unlikely languages. Nevertheless, I reread the play with some foreboding, realizing how much hung on it; if she really was a good playwright it gave *bona fides* to the other less measurable things she'd done (who can

---

* The story has been told probably once too often of Harry's grimly editing and approving a medium-bad review of this play in *Time*. I can only say that, knowing both of them, I can't conceive of him doing anything else.

really measure a congressman, or even a best-dressed woman?).

One first-class achievement was needed to clinch the rest, and *The Women* to my mind does it: comic enough to meet the Broadway demand for a laugh every thirty seconds, without ever being silly or ingratiating. In fact, it was so good that rumors started immediately that George S. Kaufman was the man under the bed this time (which Kaufman gallantly denied, on the sensible grounds that if he'd written it he'd have signed it and taken the money); everybody knew that old glamour puss couldn't write a play by herself. Ghosts were summoned from the vasty deep, stopping only at Francis Bacon.

Having read *Stuffed Shirts* and other early Clare writing, I would say that nobody else could possibly have written *The Women:* it is an author's play to an extent rare in that industry. I talked to Arlene Francis, who was in the original cast, and she told me that Clare was very cool but basically underconfident ("I think she still is"—AF) and that she was very deferential to producer Kaufman, who seemed to have amazing power over women, "I never knew why." But Miss Francis insists that George only added a few laughs and curtains, nothing substantial. Otherwise the play was essence of Clare.

I remembered Clare's having told me that Kaufman had intimidated her at the Round Table, so her submissiveness may have been a carry-over from that: although, to confuse things typically, a cache of extra-warm letters has turned up recently from, I take it, Claire Luce to George, which *Variety* attributed right away to Clare, and which would place him right in the bed itself. (Kaufman must have had his hands full in the thirties, because he also features heavily in Mary Astor's dubious diaries. Although these may have been cooked up for use in a court case, George would hardly have been cast if he wasn't the type.)

Anyway, *The Women* was a lucky play because it was highly commercial without having to try. What was on Clare's mind was on the audience's, too: the rich bitches on the stage were playing to their sisters. Everyone who had ever stolen a man, or had had one stolen, was in there—enough to pack a theater forever. The why-that's-me character, one Mary Haynes, is a basically good woman forced to learn jungle warfare in order to survive, thus offering justification to the scurviest onlookers. One pictures a playbill ad of jeweled arms pressing against tuxedo sleeves in gleeful vindication. Social Darwinism triumphant.

It's so hard to get any of yourself into a Broadway play that in her subsequent efforts Clare seems barely to have tried. (This is known as editing.) *Kiss the Boys Goodbye* (which appeared in 1938) is her plot all right, and at times her "sound," but it is smothered in one-liners, of the kind play doctors commonly rush to New Haven at the last minute. Kaufman *could* have helped with that one. The low, or high, point is the pun "viscera in Dixie," which has to be set up in such an unlikely way that it's mildly funny just for that.

Yet, if you scrape off the remorseless laughs, *Kiss* has some of the biographical value of subconscious doodling. It is a journalistic affair, a play *à clef*, almost a spin-off of *Vanity Fair*. The same people are on hand: somebody who just might be Harold Ross, a possible Heywood Broun (the rambunctious radical columnist of the thirties), and other faded photos from the magazine. The protagonist is a southern belle fairly popping her britches to play Scarlett O'Hara, or the equivalent, and we see at once that Clare's view of second-raters who hustle is merciless. Cindy Lou Bethany is a naïve kid on the make, spouting regional pieties and stopping at nothing. Her would-be exploiters range along a modest scale of decency, but they seem to be agreed that the best bet with Cindy Lou is to bed the talentless creature and get her out of town. Her task, naturally, is not to leave bed without the part.

Allowing for the requirements of comedy, this is even sourer stuff than *The Women*. Clare is kissing good-bye to more than the boys. A girl's attempt to rise in the world and the men who await her up there—in short, the whole American flesh market, and the system that made her own success possible—are cold-bloodedly skewered, like Newport. It is small wonder that the moral serious-ness of Henry Luce, for all its self-conscious, correspondence-course quality, seemed like a healthy way out of this.

If the play didn't quite kiss off Broadway too, it could surely be considered a warning kiss. Clare had ridden that world briefly like a sea horse, and was now renouncing it, like Henry V rejecting Fal-staff. As we shall see, when she later ran for Congress in Connecti-cut several Broadway luminaries went up to campaign acidly against her, as if in vengeance (though they had other, political, reasons). But the play really signals a gathering mood of disgust with herself *and* her world, which was to culminate in her semicon-fessional pieces in *McCall's* ten years later.

As if to confirm this, the play includes a quite startling piece of self-mockery. Clare and Harry had recently bought a plantation in South Carolina called Mepkin, where, among other things, Harry used to bang away harmlessly at the world's safest ducks (he loved the ritual of crouching in the blinds, but that's as far as it went). So sure enough, in *Kiss the Boys Goodbye*, we find a vulgar newspaper baron and his ditto wife gussying up a plantation, to the derision of the natives. As in *Stuffed Shirts* and *The Women*, Clare shoots herself down before anyone else can.

But like everything else in the play, this is finally just an aside, a bit of business. *Kiss the Boys Goodbye* is simply too superficial in method and plot to be a statement: it is more like an outburst of undefined spleen. One senses a puritan hangover from the Café Society binge. She was sick of that world, but hadn't found another. Harry the news tycoon could hold up that banner of Seriousness, but there really wasn't enough to it for a bright woman. Luce was no substitute for a religion. Space limitations and all that.

Her next play, *Margin for Error*, produced in 1939, escapes from all this painful probing by way of that magic hatch, World War II, in which all problems were simplified. Suddenly we, all of us, were good or bad, by accident of geography. A beastly German consul is murdered and a Jewish cop is the hero. Clare may have relished the release from self-doubt, like a general absolution before battle. At any rate, not until the final shot of the real war was fired, when good and evil dissolved into familiar patterns, did she return professionally to private complexities.

*Margin for Error* is written by an altogether simpler person than the previous plays. Although the real German embassy in Washington kicked up its heels in the Nazi manner, there was nothing in the play for even them to go to war about. As a popular entertainment, it leaves behind only a spray of anecdotes. One: it introduced Otto Preminger to the American public, and Clare swears he'd been a perfectly normal person up to then. But in playing the part of a villainous Nazi colonel, Otto began to talk funny and act funny, and that's the way you get him today, still playing one of his first Broadway parts around the clock. Take it or leave it.

The other concerns a technical bit of staging. The bet was whether you could so distract an audience that a murder could be enacted center stage with all the lights on. Clare found that a Nazi Bund rally, fully amplified and with Hitler himself speaking, did the trick. Like the period in general, that whole Busby Berkeley-to-Disney-to-Speer era of special effects, the result was a theatrical portentousness beyond any rational substance. Aside from that, *Margin for Error* is Clare's most successful attempt to get the cat up the tree and down again.

*Margin for Error* is less gaggy than *Kiss* and has a neater plot, but as a comedy-mystery it comes under the heading of carpentry, and not art. By then she was designing plays so well that they were getting perilously close to everybody else's plays. Like many American playwrights, the more she learned, the more she was in thrall to Broadway conventions—not out of weakness, but because the people who put on plays know no other.

The almost accidental power of *The Women* would have been enough to frighten many an author away from real self-expression. What may well have begun as a satire on certain types, like *Stuffed Shirts*, had ended as a timeless tableau of evil. Although it is a comedy convention from Aristophanes through Wilde to make all your characters heartless, Clare simply had too much conviction. Her heartlessness rang a bell. The beauty parlor and jewelry counter were not some *Iolanthe* fairytale, but hell itself. In an introduction to the printed version of *The Women*, Clare goes to unusual lengths to distance herself from her bitches, saying how much she herself detests them and defining them as a small predatory class, found only in New York—which would hardly account for *The Women's* extraordinary appeal in Germany and Tokyo, or the fact that it was most poignantly played in drag by a company of GI's in World War II.

This preface suggests an already well developed streak of defensiveness, or of preternatural anticipation, as if she knew what her enemies were thinking and was determined to neutralize it. For *Kiss the Boys Goodbye*, she appended a note that has baffled people ever since, including herself by now, I think. It states simply that the play is about the rise of fascism in America. I don't know *what* she was trying to ward off with that one. She also asked Heywood Broun to do the intro to the printed version, even though he may have been one of the characters and, as a real-life reviewer, had already panned it once. Broun cheerfully panned it again for her, but the curse was taken off by the invitation.

Her susceptibility to what others were thinking took a curious and ominous turn with her next introducer. Harry Luce himself did the preamble to *Margin for Error*, in which he showed neither interest nor understanding of theatrical possibilities, but treated the play as a more or less unsuccessful political tract. Clare had clearly given up on Heywood Broun and his crowd and was playing to a new jury. She was now willing to be one of the Luces, part of the Clare and Harry team.

So there's no holding him back any longer. The dazzled young husband watching quietly from the wings has suddenly marched center stage and made an announcement. "Harry didn't care for theater people," Clare explains now, "so we saw less and less of them." Thus, just like that, our pioneer gave up what she did best and began the inexorable crawl to politics. Although she took random stabs at restoring herself as a playwright, her roots had been yanked out cleanly. She began seeing the people I'd met that summer. Good, sober people. Rereading *Kiss the Boys Goodbye* gave me a by now familiar feeling about this. Was it Harry who sent Broadway packing or was it she? The play breathes the same odd mixture of admiration and contempt as *Stuffed Shirts*. The New York smarties are awful but . . . it might be fun to be one for a day, just as it might be fun to be a snotty dowager. If this seems two-faced, so is the theater itself, and Clare wouldn't have qualified as a dramatist at all if she didn't have at least two.

What is interesting is how quickly she backed away from her gift, almost as soon as she discovered it. Not that she didn't, as noted, attempt several more plays over the years: but she never again pulled out all the stops, or exposed her own psyche. It was certainly a dangerous gift for a woman in her position to have. She had written a parody of her own "type" in *The Women*, but instead of getting her off the hook, the parody was used against her. She had written the perfect Clare Luce anecdote, and it became the prototype for all Clare Luce anecdotes: partly, I believe, because the public needed a Clare Luce type to hiss at (see Epilogue), but perhaps partly because of this weird empathy of hers. Clare's bitches are fascinating, and one thinks, as one should with any good author: well, maybe she'd like to be one of those too. *"Madame Bovary, c'est moi"*—if Flaubert could "be" a provincial housewife, it was a much shorter jump for Clare to be a schemer under a hair dryer.

Since this was emphatically not what she wanted to be taken for, she did no more such powerful impersonations, but took to ingenious plotting instead—very weak tea after *The Women*. So if Harry finally shooed her show-biz friends away, it was probably not an unwelcome rescue.

Theories about who did what to whom are never harder to establish in Clare's career than at this particular point. Harry Luce was an environment all right, whether he wanted to be or not. Even if he encouraged Clare to go on with her nice plays, everything about him breathed that this was not the world's real work. The first question is, why marry a Harry Luce at all?

# CHAPTER FIVE

# *Notes on a Career -* II: *Clare and Harry, 1935-49*

According to much-polished anecdote, Harry pulled his watch on her and said, "Got to go" the first two times they met in 1935, and the third time he did not. Instead he briskly expressed his intention of marrying her forthwith, as one might announce a merger. This would certainly be a very powerful thing to do and a knockout for a romantic like Clare. But although I'm suspicious of how often such proposals turn up in memoirs, this one is as likely as most—if only because of the difficulty of holding Harry's attention.

I assume that Clare allowed the sexual magnetism to be turned on (it was seldom off in those days), which cut the preliminaries for a busy man. But the tales that quickly circulated of her seducing him in a dazzling white dress, etc., have a Victorian ring to them. People have to get into bed somehow and track suits are seldom worn. That she may have left him briefly dangling by his Puritan conscience while she took a six-month cruise to think it over also seems reasonable today, but was put down to diabolical cleverness at the time.

The possibility that there was a powerful mutual attraction hedged with normal lunges and hesitations seemed ruled out by their importance and ambition. Yet Harry was in fact precisely her type: physically, he was close enough to other men whom I know she finds interesting (although Harry photographed grimly) to suggest that their romance wasn't just power calling to power. Mentally, he was an extension of Baruch by other means: more global, but just as American, another confirmation of Mother's home truths. And morally, he was a decent man who knew his way in the jungle, like the heroine of *The Women*, like America in the world, as they both saw it.

Nevertheless, it was important for her to make clear for the record that *he* pursued *her*, because the non-record, or myth, ran all the other way. To begin with, Harry was already married and had two sons, not to mention two edifying magazines. The Other Woman was always public enemy number one in those days, whatever the circumstances; but in this case, the circumstances were bad too. Harry looked like a pillar of rectitude (an old Presbyterian trick—his sexual rectitude was to prove just about the national average) and he also looked absentminded, as if a smart woman could steal him while he wasn't looking.

Clare for her part lived in the scandal regions: a divorcee on the way up could hardly avoid one, even if she slept under armed guard. Wallis Simpson was the prototype of the day and Wallie's desperate maneuvering showed a thin-lipped world how villainous the type really was. So the record could say what it liked; the gossip had Clare reclining on a tiger skin all the way.

And, of course, she had to go and write *The Women*, which is all about husband-snatching, while the gossip mills were still spinning. Clare's motives were presumably as mixed as those of anybody's who makes a royal marriage (as crowned heads go, Luce made more sense romantically than your run-of-the-mill sheik or princeling). Just as *Vanity Fair* was the perfect job for launching herself, so was Harry the perfect husband for a second stage boost. But she *loved* him for being that, and still does. It was her Shavian dream come true—Man and Superwoman. She would consider it immoral *just* to use a man to get ahead.

What's interesting in terms of the period is that Harry's motives may have been just as complicated, and certainly anything but absentminded, yet nobody thought of him as the scheming one. Clare made a marvelous jewel for his crown, a worthy consort as he assumed his role as world leader, and a testament to his go-getting virility. His previous wife, Lila, struck me when I met her many years ago as charming and chatty but nothing like regal enough for the wife of Time Inc. For that he needed an actress, or something better than an actress.

Clare was the perfect choice for this compulsive if somewhat commonplace dreamer. She knew how Society worked as he never could, and who can calculate how much she did to make this gruff Dodsworth-like American presentable? Harry loved to learn and Clare liked to teach. She war-gamed Society like a *Time* researcher. But her real value was her contrast. The effect of them together was like an inspired clash of colors. It worked. His gruffness sparkled, her flippancy was solemnified. A wonderful couple.

Whether or not such minor art is a worthy thing in itself, it seems to be what Harry wanted in his own odd way, and he went after it as curtly and efficiently as he edited. In fact the manner of his proposal suggests a Luce memo. "Please give a yesno, Luce query soonest." Everything about his career suggests that he was an active agent, and no passive seductee. And the proof is that even after the marriage cooled as a marriage, he never tired of the ceremonial aspect of Clare. He liked being seen with the kind of woman his magazines celebrated. And he was at his absolute best as husband to the Ambassador to Italy in the fifties.

One reason for the marriage that was barely considered, because it was not so much fun, is that after six years of bachelor living Clare might have been looking for a good father for her daughter, Ann. At any rate, she got one. In no time we find Harry firing off letters to the Foxcroft School persuading that posh establishment to enroll his "daughter" Ann. From the few brief written exchanges that still exist between Luce and Ann one gets a curiously comfortable and old-shoe feeling that I myself never came close enough to Luce even to imagine. She seems to have been completely undaunted and at ease with him from the first, which took some doing on both sides—though it's possible, from his missionary ghetto upbringing, that Harry was more comfortable among females. One cryptic cable from her goes: "Your procedure in life [*Life?*] very acceptable. Love, Annie." To which Harry gravely replies: "Your solemn approval extremely encouraging and will proceed in direction indicated." That has a nice tone, I think.

Clare wanted a real family, and by God she got that too. Clare's health and whereabouts tend to be so much the centerpiece of the notes between "Annie" and "Dad" that one gets the slight feeling that they were *both* doing it—being such model family members—partly to please Clare. I can just see the old playwright handing them the parts, making the project seem exciting, pitching in herself when available. Her feeling for family was and is intense, and it is noteworthy that she did not shed her mother and brother even now, in sight of the top, but actually had Harry looking for jobs for David.

But back to business. The most diverting speculation about this mighty mating of dowries is, of course, the most cynical one. By the third and fateful third meeting, Clare had got across to Harry her plans for *Life* magazine, and in his headstrong romantic way, Luce announced, "I don't want any more babies, but if you marry me, I'll start your magazine." It is often forgotten that Clare was an accomplished editor herself and not just a dog forever walking on its hind legs (Dr. Johnson's famous comparison of which to preaching women having been applied to Clare with bone-crushing monotony). Harry might even have considered hiring her himself, if he hired women editors. As it is, more conventionally, he married her instead and hired her idea.

If "hired" is the word. Time Inc. in those days was a very stag affair and it wanted no part of the boss's wife from the first. So although Clare could send all the memos she wanted (and she is a formidable memo sender), she wasn't allowed any piece of the magazine she'd dreamed up. And with the speed of journalistic evolution, *Life* began to look less like her idea anyway. Anyone can say, "Let's have a magazine with pictures"—*that's* not an idea. There were already several *Life* lookalikes in Britain and France. So why was the lady making a fuss? Did she want credit for everything?

As it happens, her complete authorship was established in a most satisfactory way. A couple of photographers did sue *Life* for plagiarism and, in distraction, Time Inc.'s lawyers finally called in Clare as a witness. It turned out that, while *Vanity Fair* had been sinking gracefully toward oblivion back in 1933 and '34, Condé Nast asked all hands to submit dummies for possible new magazines. Clare did hers with the help of Dr. Agals, the art director, and one day a couple of photographers, who worked around the place, lit on it and made it their own. Clare rummaged in the attic, and there it was, including even the suggested purchase of *Life* itself, the moribund humor magazine. Clare, perhaps a little giddy with vindication, asked the judge, "Should I show my legs, the most beautiful in the West?" In those days you could have legs or you could start magazines, but not both. Clare had a rare chance, in a court of law, to prove you could do both.

The case was dismissed, and widely forgotten. Clare had all the satisfaction she was going to get. For whatever it tells us about men and women, about Clare and Harry, and about who won the marriage: when they got home from court, Luce said, "I never want you to mention this again."

Charles Murphy, a long-term *Time-Lifer* and student of the Luces (and author of *The Windsors*), believes that Harry's third baby, *Life*, was too much for him, the demon in the litter, Clare's baby. Up to then he had been a normal-sized editor; but with those thousands of trucks rolling every week just for him, he became the Big Fellow, virtually a principality, and more than ready for World War II.

Clare the playwright had been quite good enough for the smaller version of Luce, and she wrote her well-known plays as his wife. "When I couldn't have a magazine," says Clare of the launching of *Life*, "I said 'all right,' I'll write a play." Hence *The Women*. Harry, beneath beetle brows, was pleased as punch. He hadn't merged with Clare to liquidate her. Meanwhile, World War II watched, waited.

It was indeed the approach of war that changed all that. Luce's magazines got more serious and political, and Environment Luce clouded over with them. Clare wrote her semipolitical *Margin for Error*, but even that wasn't serious enough for Luce now. And before you can say Henry Robinson Luce, Clare was a war correspondent.

The central question, here and again and again, is the influence of masculine wishes on Clare. The balance is too intricate to define precisely: Luce was proud of her as a consort, but also proud of her as a newsmaker. As a puppet she was useless. As an independent, she would have broken up the team. There would have been no "Luces"; just a coincidence of talents. Suffice it to say of this period that he wasn't tying her to the bedpost.* The life she chose for the next few years must have been wonderfully tempting; however second-best it may seem to her now, it requires no tortured explanations.

The world of Luce, as World War II loomed up, was theatrically much more exciting than the shrunken New York stage. (In fact, the logical next move in that line would have been Hollywood, where the original *Margin for Error* would have seemed like a work of brooding originality. The feeble movie version that was made of

---

* When I mentioned Chesterton's phrase "I want to be free—to bind myself," Luce asked me to repeat it twice.

that is indication enough of what Tinseltown would have done to her.) By contrast, Harry offered her an empire at a time when most people couldn't even get a passport. The game was to see how many ways there were to enjoy being a Luce wife: from war correspondent to junketing congresswoman to fellow potentate.

Clare's war seems like a Technicolor extravaganza at this distance. As a *Life* reporter, she would turn up in France with Wallis Simpson, and then the next thing you knew she'd be in Burma with General Wingate at the start of his bloody march. Her Churchillian high spirits made it all seen rather a lark, and they contrasted bizarrely with the grim events she was covering. In fact, she says she was severely shaken by her first sight of casualties, but could see that a severely shaken woman was no use to anyone near a battlefield.

She may also have felt that cheerful pugnacity was the way you went about tackling a war. The Home Front certainly concurred with her, to judge from its zesty surface, its buy-a-bond-and-win-a-kiss hysteria. A female American Churchill may have seemed a bit much to fastidious tastes, but she shot up in the "most-admired woman" charts. One interesting sidelight to this furious activity and marked change of vocation in 1940 is that Clare's mother died in 1938. The theatrical, champagne-out-of-a-shoe side of Clare may have died with her, or at least grown paler.

And as we shall see, Clare has more than once tried to bury grief under work.

One hitch about her most-admired status was that she wasn't quite a one-man show anymore. She was the boss's wife now, which meant special treatment whether she wanted it or not (she obviously wanted it, but was too smart not to see the drawbacks). Among the letters I solicited for this project, several allude sourly to private Clare Luce latrines that had to be run up to meet her rapid advance through Italy as a congresswoman in 1944. But she mentions this herself as a particular embarrassment. Other tales have her bumping people off planes and pulling the usual scoop-getting tricks that one is resigned to in reporters but not in publishers' wives. The irony is that she was going places women didn't usually go, thus earning the applause of proto-feminists, but she was doing it as Luce's woman. The story, one might say, of her life—or one of the stories.

Meanwhile Clare the sometime New Dealer was being blooded, or was blooding herself, as a Republican spokesman ("You married Harry, you became a Republican" is her simple explanation of this vexed question) and as such she had very mixed feelings about this war she was running around in. But Clare the full-fledged pol was still two years away back in 1940.

That year she wrote *Europe in the Spring*, which certainly hints of politics to come, but is also a conscientious stab at reporting "the way it was" during the twilight of the phony war. It is a fascinating document to read today, and worth lingering over for a moment, for at least two reasons. First, it is a rich quarry of clues as to where Harry left off and Clare began in matters of foreign policy—could it possibly be that, like some medieval Pope, they divided the world in two for a while, granting Clare Europe and leaving Harry with Asia? Harry made many trips to Europe, checking the water table and any local unrest sensed in the Time Inc. Bureau, but he never came back with anything like this. Clare knew the languages and the territory, and surely the Europeans who counted would have preferred talking to her than to old Silver Tongue, even if their looks had been reversed. Second, *Europe in the Spring* is not just a stunt, another show of versatility "very good for a playwright"—but a rare specimen of satirical political analysis, whoever wrote it.

The book's angle is strictly the view from the top—although Clare does mention defensively all the maids and waiters she talked to in Paris and London, as if these represented the working class (see George Orwell's essay on Dickens for a discussion of this fallacy). Never mind. The top was where things had gone wrong in 1940, and any reporter who could get up there would have been a fool not to. One might talk in those days of the decadent French or the unimaginative English, but the citizenry itself was probably much the same as usual. Indeed, Clare emphasizes how bravely the French fought whenever they were pointed in the right direction.

Her subject is the babble of the best people as the ship goes down. She uses all the stratagems of *Stuffed Shirts* and the plays to place you at an imaginary Buñuel dinner table where the talk goes on among politicians, businessmen, faded nobility, the sort of people Luces automatically meet from China to Borneo. Germany cannot win, one hears, because it will run out of manganese; the Americans should come in right away, although we don't need them—and we certainly don't want them at the peace table; then there is the British fleet, the French *poilu*, the dikes of Holland, the rubber of Malaysia, the magic line of M. Maginot—the mental activity was unflagging, and not necessarily ill informed, but it all led in the same direction, that we don't have to do anything right now. Allied war production actually eased up in the breathing spell of

1940, like Charlie Brown on a Friday afternoon. There are so many interests to attend to in a democracy that any excuse to postpone homework is welcome. And there was even talk of holding a regular fashion season that year to show that the French had not lost their values.

Although Clare is ostensibly talking about democracy and its discontents, an innocent reader might easily suppose that she is attacking capitalism. The villains are all businessmen, big investors, men of substance. As usual, she is firing into her own camp. (She has never so effectively attacked the Left.)

With her fine ear for dialogue, Clare captures the different intellectual styles of Paris and London, and shows the different roads nations can take to the same conclusions. At times she satirizes too broadly and her people seem just silly, but generally the sound is right. Also, except for rare bursts from little Miss Knowitall, she is quite willing to admit how often she was convinced by the going sophistries. These people must have seemed so *au courant*, and she emphasizes, sometimes overemphasizes, her own innocence. What's a poor American boob to know? (Actually her entrees were enviable—and envied—and she probably got the best information around.)

Although the European opinions she records are clearly genuine, she weaves them and translates them in such a way that they resemble, in shapeliness and verve, a very effective conversation novel, in the manner of Peacock or Huxley, interrupted by real bombs. By luck or management, Clare was in Belgium when the Germans started blasting, and later she got a good look at the hysterical streams of refugees in the Paris stations. Meanwhile the men at the dinner table were gallantly regrouping their theories. The Germans were exhausted. It would take them weeks to refuel and mount another attack. In England, they were also saying, "We always lose every battle but the last one," which gives one a comfortable cushion. And everyone was saying that America would see the light just in time. . . .

Finally, as the theories toppled one by one, the talk turned ominously to treason. Since the theories had been right, and the logic was of the very best (French and all that), someone must have betrayed them. The French blamed the British and vice versa, as usual, and both blamed the Belgians, but this lacked the nourishment of chewing on one's own. So the search for scapegoats began, obscuring in Clare's view the search for lessons. If it could all be blamed on old Pétain or someone, the eternal dinner guests could be excused until next time.

Clare's avowed mission was to bring back something that America could use, and this did not include the heads of French politicians. So she scavenged for general principles among the ruins, rather short-changing, by her standards, the factor of individual responsibility. This was a tactic of convenience, not a change of heart, and it certainly didn't apply when she later got round to Roosevelt. But she was searching for a sort of *principia democratica*, an abstract of democracy's strengths and weaknesses that would apply *anywhere*.

In order to do this, she makes the common émigré mistake of applying European models to America, and it doesn't quite work— although one could undoubtedly find the same dinner parties. French inactivity in 1940 was bizarre, American understandable. The situations simply could not be made to look the same. At one point Clare briefly raises the specter of a Nazi invasion across the Atlantic, and the unlikelihood of that, in a pre-missile era, slackens the book's overall force. (Her own return to America took a full day's flying time.) *Europe in the Spring* had already made all the case it could for American preparedness, but Clare tried to stretch it just a little bit further.

The book also seems to make a case for direct American intervention; but while one is awaiting the details, she veers off into a wild list of questions of the kind she used to ask Harry at dinner. The reader is asked to consider every conceivable alliance, including one with Japan, in order presumably to get America thinking; which is laudable at any time but not quite what we were waiting for. Do we fight or don't we?

This slight shyness about intervention indicates the delicate position Clare and other East Coast Republicans* occupied in 1940. On the one hand, this group was just about to maneuver the proto-internationalist Wendell Willkie past isolationist Robert Taft at the Republican Convention; but on the other, they would then have to campaign against the dreaded Roosevelt, who was suspected of dragging us into war.

The solution, always available to the powerless, was to accuse

---

* Historical identities are never quite satisfactory. But the Luce wing in 1940 does parallel the later Rockefeller, Eastern Seaboard, wing: what the Republicans somewhat puzzlingly call their moderates.

FDR of intervening wrong, while never quite admitting that he should be intervening at all. Thus in *Europe in the Spring* Clare strikes up the theme that we don't have a *bad* foreign policy, because we don't have *any* foreign policy (a pensée she would later embroider a whole speech around when she got to Congress). This, it will be noted, evades the question elegantly.

But anyone who reads the whole book will have no doubt that Clare was fairly itching to take off the gloves and paste Herr Hitler a good one in the chops. Clare hated nazism every bit as much as she has ever hated communism, which is not invariably the case on the Right. She tells me she refused to meet Hitler in 1937 because she was afraid that, womanlike, she would smile nervously, and she wasn't taking any chances. I myself remember in the fifties a particularly florid businessman at Clare's Ridgefield house announcing at table that we'd backed the wrong side in World War II, no doubt thinking to please his hosts but being received instead like an untimely fart.

Clare had no doubts about the sides in World War II. *Margin for Error,* produced on its eve, was a premature anti-Nazi comedy, not precisely a searing attack, given the form, but certainly sincere enough. The central confrontation, between a Nazi consul and a wise-guy Jewish cop who speaks for civilization, authentically expressed the upstart side of Clare, which has not changed an inch.

One of her influences by then was Winston Churchill, who, it goes without saying, had posed for *Vanity Fair*, after being introduced by Bernard Baruch, that introducer of champions. Churchill had wanted then and there to arrange an English marriage for her as her mother had tried before him. Unfortunately it was to be with one of his sons, the incredible Randolph, who repelled even Evelyn Waugh and who could easily have emptied George Brokaw's golf trophies at a sitting.

Winston himself, whom Hilaire Belloc once described as "that Yankee adventurer," was just up Clare's alley, though, and many of her Cold War alarums are simply translations of Churchill into American. If she could have, she would have lobbied transatlantically to have him made Prime Minister in the mid-thirties—she certainly talked to English friends about it—which put her squarely in the anti-Nazi camp while England slept (at least the top part slept; the middle part where I hung out as a tot was scared witless from 1937 on). Since her other huge influence, Luce himself, was also smitten by Churchill, *Time-Life* became practically the latter's house organ, and he was a shoo-in for *Time*'s Man of the Half-Century in

1950. The combined Luce politics were far from any sort of nativist right wing. They were the Yankee adventurer back in an American setting, with British imperialism shading into American, well, leadership.

All these immediate political considerations surely weakened Clare's credentials as a prophet, if that's what she wanted to be. *Europe in the Spring* is a strong, evocative book, and considering the speed with which it was written (five weeks), an amazingly astute briefing for Harry and the country for which Harry stood. It is easily her best claim as a global thinker.

Yet it is dated in the wrong sense for me by that slight clanking of domestic politics in the margin. While Clare was still feverishly working on the manuscript, Harry announced that they were going to have dinner with Wendell Willkie. "Wendell who?" Clare says she almost said; or at least "Wendell why?" She was still so immersed in Europe that she'd missed the rapid surge of the Indiana dark horse in Republican politics.

The rest of her book might have been better if she'd never found out Wendell who. As it was, she went to dinner and heard this Willkie expounding on the need for a good businessman, a real administrator—"like you, Harry"—for next President. Clare told him he was crazy: no one would nominate a businessman in the endless wake of the depression. Harry kicked Clare smartly under the table, but she persisted and Harry distastefully kicked her again. On the way home he explained that the businessman Willkie had in mind was not Harry at all but himself.

Before she knew it, Clare found herself giving a speech for Willkie's favorite businessman. It had not been intended as a speech at all, but as a letter to the paper rebuking Dorothy Thompson for endorsing FDR. But Wendell saw it first and persuaded her that it was too fine for that. So she delivered it full blast in Carnegie Hall: and what might have been an average nasty letter was amplified into a legendary feud.

Talk about your fatal glass of beer: Clare still remembers a sweet little old lady in the front row, nodding and smiling every time Clare gave it to Thompson. "I became more and more vitriolic," says Clare, egged on by this harpy (who, of course, attends all political rallies). The long-range effect on Clare's career was drastic, but one immediate result was, as I say, the slight weakening of a very fine book.

As an account of the Fall of France, Alistair Horne, perhaps the leading historian on that subject, calls *Europe in the Spring* just about the truest rendering one can find. But every now and then the strains of a campaign document can be heard. The book is date-lined July 1940, the month in which Willkie took the Republican Convention by storm, at least partly due to the Luces. And it is dedicated to Harry, a sort of symbolic signing on. Thus the Sage gives ground to the adversary journalist, and the journalist, in turn, yields to the all-out partisan politician of 1942. When Clare says now she wishes she'd never got into politics at all, it could be this descent into Lucification that she is talking about.

*Europe in the Spring* sits on my desk with a preposterously glam-orous picture of Clare on the jacket, no doubt a good selling point in 1940, but fatally undercutting the serious work within. It was tough enough to concentrate in her sizzling presence. So why re-mind readers that they are listening to a beautiful woman? Why hedge one's bets like this? Anyway, it sold a lot of copies.

I believe it would have done so with a picture of King Farouk on the jacket. Besides the virtues already mentioned, *Europe in the Spring* is a better mix of substance and entertainment than she had ever achieved at *Vanity Fair*. It is full of funny sketches, including a devastating one of an old friend, Margaret Case of *Vogue*, who is portrayed as a braying ninny whose gravest concern, outside of her excess baggage, is the beastly effect of war on the fashion industry: just the kind of thing some people used to say about the author herself until she'd subdued them with sheer talent in her plays. Clare might say that she was just fooling around, but if so it's the way a doberman pinscher fools around. She did clear it with her friend Maggie ("I *love* it, darling"), who didn't grasp, until her friends told her, how devastating it was. But all that the public could see was Clare scratching another woman's eyes. (When Mar-garet Case committed suicide promptly on her eightieth birthday, she left a note saying that she loved Clare, long since forgiven, more than anyone.)

Of Clare's further wartime reporting, it was probably most no-table for its enterprise. Her greatest coup was a photograph of the Flying Tigers, who, holed up somewhere in Burma, were consid-ered next to impossible to get to; but the photo appeared in *Life* under someone else's name. Even without such discouragements, she soon decided that her beloved (from *Vanity Fair* days) photogra-phy took a different kind of attention from writing, that you couldn't really think story and picture simultaneously. If you were waiting for Mahatma Gandhi to say something funny, you couldn't worry about the lighting. So she didn't try to add "great woman photographer" to her bulging catalog.

As a reporter, she was willing to go anywhere, as she had been in the different circumstances of Prohibition. But her situation and temperament decreed that she continue to top-people hop, particularly among generals, her new favorites. She is very funny about Douglas MacArthur, that mountebank of genius, and tells of making trade-offs with him, e.g., tacitly agreeing not to mention the subject of dyed or thinning hair in exchange for some military scoop or other. Although she has an old-fashioned weakness for pear-shaped oratory, she found MacArthur frankly incredible, because he talked exactly the same way in private, a distinction she is sensitive to. Silhouetted against a Pacific sky and using every effect but organ music, MacArthur told how one man and one man alone stood between America and Asian world dominance, total and forever. Even Harry, with his gluttony for greatness, found this a bit rich for his blood. "He's either a great fraud or a genius," he stopped the elevator to mutter. "Probably both."

In early 1942, Clare made a global sweep covering some 75,000 miles, with a view to doing for Asia and Africa what she had already done for Europe. But without the languages and feel for the culture, it was just not possible. Her Asia seems to have been packed with occidentals, such as Generals Stilwell and Alexander and Sir Stafford Cripps, presumably as much at sea as she was, and with blarneying orientals like Nehru and Chiang, whose respective lines she didn't have the background to judge.

Fortunately no very subtle judgments were called for: Burma, China, India, all needed help instantly, and she concentrated on hollering for that. She had seen enough action (courageously, of course: courage is *naked* willpower) to convey very graphically the flavor and smell of it. In the few pieces I've seen, she modestly laid off the heavy analysis and prophecy in favor of straight reporting, which she did pretty well (especially good on towns and villages under fire). But *Life* did reject some other submissions because of "political differences concerning the Orient,"* which raises intriguing questions. Did she at that time dare to differ from Harry on the subject? or was there a Maoist saboteur in the *Time-Life* boiler room? or, more likely, was *Life* simply rationing her contributions

---

* Faye Henle, *Au Clare de Luce* (Brattleboro, Vt.: Daye, 1943). Although I shall be taking this book to task a little later, it contains some useful material on the first war years.

out of house pride, and using the gentlest excuse that lay to hand?

I find it hard to believe that she ever fought with Harry on this particular turf, especially if he'd ceded her Europe. There was simply no doubt when I met the Luces that Harry was the Asian expert around there, with Clare tagging along like a Chinese bride. Prior to Harry, there is no record of excessive orientalism in Clare's life. Yet at Ridgefield I often felt as if I was walking into a pagoda and should at least take my shoes off. It was Harry's mania and it was best not to mess with it.

The fact was, you simply couldn't marry Harry "Chink" Luce without taking out Chinese citizenship—not precisely from China, of course, but from the mythical kingdom of Yankee-poo, where the twain of East and West meet around the clock. Luce, son of missionary, did not dream of being a Chinaman, but only a friend to China-men. As with Kipling and so many Englishmen, there was a super-glamorous role of go-between: the manifest Westerner who sits in the lotus position and talks three dialects. Westernized Chinese like Chiang Kai-shek and Chinafied Americans like Luce seemed in those days to form a bridge between civilizations, but it was a bridge without shores. The actual America and the actual China were as far apart as ever. Luce and Chiang were suspended beautifully in midair.

Beautifully, because what ended as the China lobby—a dyspeptic rearguard action against reality in the fifties—began as a very attractive dream, a merger of high Chinese culture and Western political savvy with Christianity as the glue. Christian missionaries are now largely remembered for bearing trousers and gloom, but in fact many of them made an effort to assimilate to local cultures beyond anything attempted by more secular Westerners. It was their pride that Christianity could do this, because that is what it was for. Luce himself could not have assimilated if he'd wanted to. The thought of Luce's acting any part is funny, even this one where he had a head start by virtue of birth. Try as he might, he could not be a born-again Chinese, except of the most Presbyterian sort. Even in oriental robes and a pigtail, he would have looked like the same old Harry. Clare, on the other hand, could have become a passable Chinese wife. She struck up a close acquaintanceship with Madame Chiang Kai-shek (who could, of course, "do" an American perfectly) largely out of curiosity, I think, and she still tells more stories about her than the rest of China put together. It was as if she had studied the Madame to see how it was done; and no doubt the Madame was studying her right back. It was one of the great match-ups of the century.

At this point, Clare's interest was still perceived to be what used to be called feminine, i.e., a fascination with manners and the little watch springs of personality that Harry couldn't even see. The eye that brought us *Stuffed Shirts* and *The Women* was now trained on bigger fish, but seeing the same things. Clare's passion to be taken seriously had to temper itself somewhat into "the woman's angle," despite the credentials established by *Europe in the Spring*.

Clare the would-be Spengler and Clare the Maugham-like story finder hit on an accommodation, by bouncing from the big picture to the small one, turning a country into a single person and vice versa. France, say, could be portrayed as an idea, a woman, a love of logic personified (big picture), or an individual like Count Ciano, smooth and evasive, could *be* Italy (small picture). This would become a trademark, the thing I had noted at the dinner table: at best, it rolled out a dazzling array of new perspectives and groupings—I can see why so many committees wanted her along; at worst, it was just pretty pictures—which is why they wanted her perhaps as an advisor rather than a chairman. A writer of fictions can seldom hope to be more than a wise jester.

Either way, wise or just clever, Clare suited Harry, who liked his ideas nice and large, and who had his own stake in a dramatic world (news magazines, of course, often have to invent one). Harry *had* married a playwright, after all, and there are no accidents in a Calvinist's life. Luce presumably encouraged Clare in her dual mode of thinking, big to little and back, because he found it fruitful. It limbered up his own slightly stiff imagination and gave it a hundred themes to play with. To have such fertility around the house was a godsend for an editor.

Reflecting on Clare's lament in 1949 that she had lost her talent, I wonder now whether converting to the Church might have had less to do with it than converting to Luce. Just having a walking news magazine around the house would affect one's way of looking at things after a bit: e.g., is so-and-so worth a cover story?—he is if he Represents a Trend. And Clare's mind was all too happy providing these links. To hear the two of them talk while they were jigsawing was to catch them in their essence, with Clare free-associating cannily (a contradiction I know) and Harry grunting it all in. But whatever the pluses and minuses as regards her writing talent (surely she talked too much material away), her marriage

stimulated Clare into the other accomplishments that made her famous. Harry released *at least* all that was second-best in people, and
many old *Time* hands feel that they could have done a lot worse.

Of course, Clare was not a *Time* hand, but to marry Luce was to
marry his blue pencil: they were one and inseparable. And it is
tempting to say that she might have made a better writer if she'd
married a better editor. But she wouldn't have made such a good
story. After *Europe in the Spring* the writing days dwindled and the
public self grew. Once again, as soon as she got on top of something, she tried something else. She plugged on with her writing
and still plugs—but without the lunatic dedication it requires. Instead, the lecture platform became an uneasy compromise with her
early dreams. And in 1942, she entered politics, that ultimate cor-
rupter of style, and went national. Undoubtedly she was propelled
into it by her tongue. That first speech for Willkie led to another
and another, as Clare discovered, like so many writers before and
since, the joys of the quick payoff, of not having to wait months and
years for a response from the crazy little old lady out there. Also
the actress Clare was groomed to be finally had someplace to go.
The distorting factor was that so many of her first speeches were
political, so that the various other things you can do with rhetoric
besides sneering, browbeating, and sounding noble had to come
later. Although speaking was to be half of each of her careers from
now on, I honestly believe we will never know how good her oratory might have been with saner origins.

Anyway, it was plenty good enough for her purpose, which
was to get elected twice by a whisker, in 1942 and '44, in a predomi-
nantly Democratic Fourth District in Connecticut,* and with no
more than the usual whispers about electoral fraud the second time
around. (A couple of correspondents mentioned these to me triumphantly as if every dead cat could be brought to Clare's door. But if
there was hanky-panky—hard to believe in Connecticut politics—it
surely didn't need any help from her.)

Harry undoubtedly encouraged the move from Broadway to
Washington—it could hardly have happened without him. So what
did the old boy have in mind this time?

"To get me out of the house," says Clare wryly. But what Luce
expected out of politics is never quite as clear as that, because he

---

* Fairfield County is and was very rich but also very industrial, since it contains Danbury and Bridgeport. By what seems to me a quite strikingly uninteresting coincidence,
Clare's stepfather, Dr. Austin, had also won this seat for a term in 1938.

probably never knew himself. He was, if ever there was one, the kind of boy who dreams of becoming President someday, and he may have thought of Clare as a sort of feeler in that direction, to see how the country really responded to Luces. But of course, Clare was too much of a one-woman turn to be a feeler for anyone, and he must have known it. More likely, he just wanted to see what would happen. He was a curious man, in both senses.

The boys at Time Inc. (there were no girls to speak of) emphatically did not want Mrs. Luce to become a congresswoman and disgrace the magazine. Which, considering that they didn't want her to edit *Life* magazine either, leaves one wondering what—leaving aside locker room jocularities—they did want her to do. The managing editor, Ralph Ingersoll, even complained that she was taking Harry away at 5 P.M. every day, robbing them of his golden night hours. And there was a rumor that some effort may have been made later by a Time Inc. executive to block the Luces' move to Ridgefield from the handier location of Greenwich, on the same ground. So even sitting home doing nothing was objectionable.

For a woman bent on making a career, the *Time* connection was as booby-trapped as any other big-company connection. Clare could thenceforth count on a certain number of back-room hecklers with a way for words, whose influence on Harry might reasonably be expected to grow as his infatuation with her cooled. Whether the pressure on him came from without or within, Clare now says that "for a publisher's wife, I got less support from the publisher than any character in history. . . ." Harry was proving a point, which was that he could be objective, even about his wife.

"I was the chin that Harry led with," adds Clare. The outrageous young woman could float Harry's ideas in Congress, and if they didn't work—well, that's old Clare for you. She seemed so confident that one assumed she was independent through and through. Her besotted duffer of a husband would tolerate just about anything from her, was the feeling. In turn, the magazine may have felt that *it* was the chin that *Clare* was leading with: there were grumbles on Capitol Hill that one couldn't attack Clare without getting dumped on in *Time*. Which leaves us with at least two chins, leading with each other, which may not be far from the truth. However, Clare now insists, "As a practical matter, since he [Harry] committed more sins against more people, if they want to call them that, than I ever did, I got jeered for his errors." Self-serving perhaps, but consider (a) that the old duffer was besotted like a fox and wasn't accustomed to losing at *anything*, and (b) he had, in the *Time* magazine of the forties, one of the major irritants of all time at his command—as if Clare couldn't make enough trouble all by herself.

If he had any more specific political use for Clare, it can only be deduced from scattered results. Like every politician, she had to compromise so much to get elected that it is hard to tell the one or two issues that really mattered to her: the ones that define her politically. For instance, she wooed the Connecticut labor unions zealously, and with what sounds surprisingly like conviction. She called for a soak-the-rich tax scale to the level of confiscation in order to pay for the war. She actually spoke out for more shortages rather than fewer (hard to tell which constituency *that* was aimed at), without of course laying a glove on her new friend Labor. She made uncalled-for pitches for black rights and that hardy perennial, Red Indian rights (not a big issue in Connecticut). She even voted against the Dies Committee (later HUAC), perhaps on aesthetic grounds. These were not your typical Republican positions, and in fact there were those who feared that the Luces were trying to liberalize the party under the mossbacks' noses and produce virtually a new GOP (the far Right distrusted the Luces almost as much as the Left did in those days). All that can be said for sure is that Clare wanted to win the war any way she knew how, right, left, or around corners.*

However, there remain a few items that define Clare's two terms, besides the War and the voters: both economically and geopolitically she had her own fish to fry. The actual go-between who talked Clare into running for Congress in 1942†—and not just talked, but guided her first steps—was Sam Pryor, a vice-president of Pan American Airways, and the affable chap I met at dinner on the infamous night of the dinner jacket. Sam was a Yale man, as was his boss Juan Trippe, and Luce always hit it off swimmingly with Yale men. Time Inc. correspondents used to fly Pan Am as a matter of course, and the magazine itself gave Trippe one of its more fulsome cover stories, if one can compare those rich outpourings.

It was all quite open and accepted, a routine exchange of services. What was just a little unusual was Clare's maiden speech in

---

* Clare now says, "I was just a regular East Coast liberal, who hated Soviet Russia." This simplifies a bit, but is as good an opinion as any.

† A local pol called Albert P. Morano had been after Clare to run for some time. I met Morano later, and judged him to be a good-natured, immensely decent workhorse who would do anything for Clare. But as a power behind the throne he just didn't fit.

Congress in 1943. Everybody remembers the word "globaloney" from that speech, but Clare still wins bets on what it refers to. Most of her bettors assume that she was attacking Henry Wallace and whatever form of world federation he was plugging that month, and it costs them a dollar each time. What she was attacking was Henry Wallace and *Freedom of the Skies*. The sublime Henry was recommending that after the war everybody be allowed to fly over everything and land on anybody, and Clare pointed out, among other things, that this would cut the throat of our own air industry. Foreign planes could set up their own routes here and charge what they liked, and Americans would be undersold, as they already had been in the cargo ship business. As time has since shown, a government will cheerfully subsidize an airline if it drums up peripheral business, and Clare's speech was much more practical than the breezy one that people think they remember.

Even so, the cream pies flew at once: to propose any kind of postwar air policy was considered unfriendly, if not downright Yankee imperialist. "Smart," said Lady Astor, the Clare Luce of England, "in the way that a very stylish and ridiculous hat is smart." Of course, Clare's speech became the common sense of the next few years. But at the time, it was considered strictly a blow for Harry's American Century, and perhaps it was that, too. But more immediately, it was a blow for Sam Pryor. Because in those days, Pan Am *was* the American air industry, or hoped to be, and Clare had wasted no time in stating its case for it.

"There may have been a little trade-off there," said Clare mildly when I dug up the speech in the Congressional Record and taxed her with it in 1977. She was a working politician (though a bit of an absentee at times—she had to spend time with her daughter, Ann, who was now enrolled at Stanford) with a constituency—several in fact—and she never forgot it, even in her most abstract foreign policy speeches. One of her constituencies was the blue-collar Catholics of Connecticut, and her early warnings about Russia were very much aimed at that, as well as at Pan Am and Harry. The rape of Central Europe would start with the churches, so immigrant Catholics formed a natural anti-Communist lobby. That this lobby was later led grunting off into the woods by Joe McCarthy does not affect the reasonableness of its origins. Clare's speeches provide a heartbreaking record of the speed and smoothness with which pro-Russian governments slipped into place in Poland, Hungary, Czechoslovakia, so that there was precious little to give away by the time we allegedly did so at Yalta and Potsdam. The author of *Europe in the Spring* could be pardoned for imagining a rerun to the East.

Of course the circumstances were different. It was not, as it looked, a simple question of Reds in high places slipping nations under the table to Stalin: the immediate alternative to the Soviet puppets seemed to be the kind of reactionary Christian regimes that had not held the line in the first place, and there was precious little time or strength now to build up model Christian Democratic parties as the Russians rolled through and their stooges set up shop. But to "premature anti-Stalinists" like Clare it looked as if we didn't even want to try. Elements in our government were quite happy with what we got.

In her campaigns, her worst moments (like everybody's), she attacked a phantom "Broadway to Browder" axis of New Dealers, which suggests to me not only that she was getting even with her old profession, but that she saw the value of this line of demagoguery before her time.

I've since discovered that this same line was very popular with the whole Thomas Dewey campaign *apparat* in 1944, which realized, as HUAC would later, that dragging in show biz, however irrelevant, sells tickets. So Clare did not initiate this bit of business: she was simply the last person who should have used it. Anyway, in her congressional speeches I found no special whiff of the witch-hunt, though I'll admit to dozing off over those worthy volumes. With or without witches, it was terribly hard to get people's attention as the end of the war came in view. The American psyche was overextended and had to some degree managed to shed the Russian front as a concern, except insofar as it would meet us in Berlin someday, and our postwar planning reflected, or took advantage of (depending on your point of view), this indifference. Clare's jeremiads disappeared quietly into the record.

Nevertheless, they stand up as the most impressive contributions of her congressional career. Revisionists may argue that her warnings were as empty as Foster Dulles's threats in the fifties, and that life with Stalin would have been a lot easier if we hadn't even pretended we could meddle in his sphere of influence. And it is true that the Luces tended perennially to exaggerate (like JFK himself) America's willingness to go to war in unlikely places, and to overestimate the strength of our friends in those places.

But everything cannot be judged by Vietnam. There was then an unspoken feeling among many liberals that everything in poor countries that was not communist was probably moribund. Clare argued, contrariwise, that this might not apply to the evolved nations of Eastern Europe. Her speeches dug up what evidence she could to suggest that impressive pro-Western and anti-Russian passions in Central Europe (which was not really a medieval slum) were simply waiting to be tapped, before Stalin got a toehold.

Whether they should have been is a question for another book, in fact many other books, but Clare's case was reasonable, sophisticated, and far from being right-wing rant. No doubt this was just the kind of congresswoman that Luce wanted, but there is no need to look for his hand back there: her foreign policy was consistent with everything she had ever written, down to the most frivolous plays. The spunky little guy, with whom she so oddly identifies, must be encouraged to fight the latest bully. If one reason must be adduced for her political career, this is probably it.

But this was not the kind of show that people wanted, and deplored, from Clare. They wanted their globaloney, and they wanted a brassy interloper, and that is still what they remember about her. In 1944, Clare played into their hands with her famous "GI Joe and GI Jim speech," keynoting the Republican Convention. Joe was the guy who comes back with brass bands, Jim is the one who doesn't. Jim died for our political sins, and lies in an unmarked grave.

In wartime this was incendiary stuff. To blame the politicians for our boys' deaths was considered tasteless beyond discussion. Since it seemed so likely to be true, it could only hurt the war effort, which was the ultimate sin of the moment. And the melodramatic device of the name Jim seemed an example of misplaced cleverness: it jerked tears in a way that made you want to jerk them back immediately.

The tinniness of the speech stems partly from the contradiction in her wartime position. She was, as you'll recall, an internationalist herself, one of those suspect eastern Republicans who would most likely have found their way into the war under Willkie, and would have owed GI Jim as many apologies as anybody; but Clare also maintained that FDR had "lied us into war," making him the sole culprit. She now says she would like to apologize to Roosevelt, because lying was clearly the only way to get us there. And even in 1944, she did add that if FDR had simply led us into war through the front door, everything would have been okay. But for all her complaints about being misunderstood, she must have known which part of the sentence contained the dynamite. She was calling Roosevelt a warmonger at a time when people were delirious about his war. Presumably she borrowed this lofty isolationist sentiment to block Roosevelt's leftward drift: but it was a funny way to do it. A more personal motive must at least be considered.

In *The Powers That Be,* David Halberstam describes dinners at Hyde Park in which "Roosevelt had treated Clare cavalierly as just a young, pretty (silly) thing," which must have peeved both her and Harry. Later, FDR antagonized Luce even more by canceling a proposed tour of Harry's through the Pacific theater. The history of Roosevelt's snottiness ("haughtiness" is too grand a term for such preppy one-upmanship) has never, I think, been properly evaluated. Its effect on Irish-Americans alone, because they were then at the cutting edge of sensitivity, like career women—in short, the Age of John O'Hara—is worth a note: Al Smith, James Farley, Joe Kennedy, and others all fell out with FDR at various times, and maybe they were political deadwood anyway. But the same high-handed Wasp confidence that saw us through war and depression was guaranteed to get under Celtic skins sooner or later. In fact it is not too farfetched to guess that even Father Coughlin's fascist rages had an FDR base (he had once been a New Deal supporter).

It was Roosevelt's manner as much as anything that made him seem like a potential dictator. So Clare, as a vulnerable woman, reacted to him on the two levels of personal pique and political alarm. She had gone to Washington with the open intention of "helping the President to think." But when she tried to do so at a reception for freshmen representatives, favoring jolly Franklin with her latest political ideas, FDR did not goggle like most men, but simply asked, "How's Henry?" Clare remarked later that Franklin's manners had been every bit as bad as hers. So somewhere in this tangle of vanity and realpolitik, the GI Jim speech pops up.

Clare returns to the subject quite frequently. Her rationale now is that she *knew* FDR was dying and must be beaten by fair means or foul. But the effect was that she was nearly defeated herself in her 1944 campaign for reelection, as various Celebrities for Roosevelt, such as Dorothy Parker and Clifton Fadiman, swarmed into Connecticut and stumped her district denouncing her. Edna Ferber, her fellow playwright, was particularly vituperative, as if it took a playwright to denounce a playwright.* Attacking Roosevelt was a losing proposition that year and Clare only made it worse by finally saying outright what she really wanted to say, i.e., that FDR was a dying man. "If there'd been any doubt about it, I wouldn't

---

* Clare says that she made it up with Ms. Ferber years later under a hair dryer. According to Clare (and she makes a circumstantial case for it) she made it up with just about everybody, after she became a Catholic.

have said it," she says. But the now-famous conspiracy of silence was too much for her. Roosevelt's health was practically an article of patriotic faith, like the valor of our boys and the rightness of our cause, and to question it was gross, subversive, and personally repulsive. What was one to do?

Clare had stumbled or marched into the role expected of her: that of Republican hatchet, or Nixon, which means taking on a prepackaged list of enemies. (And who better than a bitchy woman for this work?) And once you've started on that you might as well keep on attacking. One difference between her and Nixon, which may or may not recommend her to one, is that she seemed to be having fun doing it. She was still comparatively new at this inflammatory stuff and she fell on it with glee, laying on the irony and woe like a beginning chef at the spice rack. Roosevelt himself had established an atmosphere of rough and tumble, of political horseplay, and Clare seemed only to be playing him at his own game. They made, in retrospect, a rather beguiling comedy team, in a grim period. "Clear it with Sidney" was her tag line for FDR, Sidney Hillman being the venerable Labor Leader whom Roosevelt had coopted for the war effort. But this pleasantry was taken by some to be anti-Semitic—a probable case of Harry's sins being visited on her. (Harry was so spooked by his reputation for anti-Semitism that one day years later he came home with a big grin to announce that he'd found a brilliant Jew in his organization named Henry A. Grunwald, who would someday get the monkey off his back.)

The context of wartime Capitol Hill is hard to recapture now. The freshman congresswoman had been greeted right off with an oafish gallantry out of Gilbert & Sullivan, and henceforth could scarcely be mentioned without some coy reference to her beauty and charm (needless to say, nothing like that ever happened to Nixon). A note of frivolity was set, so that she could say the most awful things without drawing any real blood to speak of. Even when a hissing villain appeared—a resentful namesake called Claire Hoffman of Michigan, who "sewed his pockets shut so he wouldn't give anything away"—she could congratulate him on coming from a long line of distinguished bachelors and bring down the gallery.

Although she played the part meticulously, even down to the sensible clothes and the sensible hours, there was no way she could pass for an average congressman. The Washington press corps, especially its women, sniped at her from the very first (she was late for a press conference), then later tried to cut her down to congres-

sional size by ignoring her. Although she explained tartly that she
was not in Washington to add to her "collection," the local professionals obviously thought otherwise.

But it didn't really matter what they thought. Because Clare
had a national constituency, without having to go look for it, from
the day she arrived. She had but to open her mouth on any topic
whatever for a torrent of (largely irrelevant) mail to come flying her
way, from people who just wanted to talk to a woman or a celebrity
or both. As Congresswoman to the Nation, she was bound to mad-
den some of her less colorful colleagues, whose only real weapons
were condescension and gruff indignation.

When she proposed, as what freshman on the Hill has not, that
something be done about the seniority system on the committees,
the little lady from Broadway was clearly talking through her cha-
peau; but when she innocently asked to sit on the Foreign Relations
Committee, she was being insufferably arrogant. The fact that she
had more experience in that area than most of the committee put
together was neither here nor there. She had come to Washington,
as she went everywhere, to do something, not just sit there: but
everything she tried to do was construed as either more trophy
hunting or as an insidious plot to further Harry's ideas: to be suspected of both at once must be tiring.

This is not to say that Clare had no allies and wouldn't have
picked up more. She was an effective speaker to have on your side,
and she guaranteed you a national audience. But to have cracked
the inner circle would have taken more time than she had. She
could have become a star immediately, but power takes a lifetime,
and even a power-mad publisher could hardly have expected much
from a freshperson congressperson. So she might as well enjoy
herself.

Politics, it goes without saying, was an extension of theater to
Clare, and as usual there are not too many parts open to women.
Her choice of Witty Hit Woman was the most entertaining she
could have chosen—as opposed, say, to Margaret Chase Smith's
Rock of Integrity. Unfortunately, gibing at Roosevelt brought her
not only enemies but friends: in this case, a jeering rancorous gallery, along with a few sensibles, which attached itself to Clare in the
forties and has never really let go. They are a dismally easy crowd
to play to, roaring at everything halfway nasty, whatever its quality.
But an audience is an audience and a trouper must work.

The groups that invite you to lecture affect the tone of your act
after a while, and the public Clare became more of a partisan politi-

cian than she now would like to have been. At some low point in the war, a clerical correspondent swears he heard her say, "I'll dance on Franklin Delano Roosevelt's grave"—there were several graves in her life just then and she might hysterically have wanted FDR in one of them—which may be why she now regrets going into politics at all.

Because two other things were happening to her during those years on the Hill that were pulling her away from her new Dragon Lady role. One was that she was developing a slight contempt for politics as such—arrived at backwards from the discovery that politicians themselves were so second-rate (hence the offhand way she treated Congressmen Brewster and Martin that Summer of mine): and if they were, there must be something wrong with their business. "The receptacle of all second-rate talents," she quotes Count Ciano as saying about his own political career. "He could have included me," she adds. (After a glittering career in New York, Washington is likely to have this plonking effect on most anyone; imagine how long Dorothy Parker would have lasted.) "A politician can never admit a mistake," as she told me in 1949; and even if this were the only dishonesty involved, it would be enough to unravel civil discourse.

The other thing was that, while her reputation for nastiness still grew wild as a weed, she was consciously trying to be nicer. She had once announced that her natural rival, the journalist Dorothy Thompson, was "the only woman who ever conducted her menopause in public," and it had blown instantly into such a dream feud that press agents could have kept it going forever. Both women did their bit to fan it before they saw what was happening. Back in 1940, Clare challenged Thompson to a debate and the latter thanked her, in reply, for offering her a part in *The Women*, but said she wasn't the type. So they were beautifully matched.

Alert too late to the public taste for hair-pulling women, Clare determined to patch it up with Thompson and all future Thompsons. She made a mutual nonaggression pact with the formidable Dorothy, which did not prevent the gag-writing community from distributing fresh insults between the two ladies periodically. Even when Thompson took out a paid ad for Clare in her 1942 campaign, people thought it was a trick.

Clare made similar pacts with her fellow congresswomen: not only to avoid downright insult, but not to comment on each other's speeches at all. It may reasonably be assumed that nobody noticed the sudden sweetness. Clare's reputation as a firebrand burned on

its own juice by now. But when you think about it, it *is* quite a sacrifice, if you're good at it and people expect it anyway, to pass up a
cruel wisecrack on principle: it must be almost as hard as the "little
way" of St. Thérèse.

The operatic climax of her whirl through Congress was a jun-
ket she took through Italy in 1944 with a group of fellow pols,
where by accident or design she stole the limelight. Your average
congressman of the era was, if one is to believe Will Rogers, not
much competition for a pretty woman, or even for a pet rock, and it
would have taken a determined effort to keep *out* of the limelight.
And there is no reason to suppose she tried: none of the others
would have. But it's hard to imagine a war-weary soldier lighting
up at the sight of a congressman. So if Generals and GI's preferred
having their photos taken with her rather than with Representative
Nurd of Plainsville, who was she to insist on quotas? "You can't
name one of them [generals] who didn't say, 'Let's have a picture
taken,' " she says; and their word was her command.

Unfortunately her fellow-travelers also had a vested interest in
publicity, and they had to feel that Clare was using her looks and
connections unduly to beat them into print. She did in a sense
double as a species of USO camp show, and soldiers have a duty to
make a demented fuss over visiting women however tired they may
feel about it. Anyway, a glance at the picture magazines shows
Clare marching through Italy with that infuriating gusto of hers,
giving snappy quotes when people got tired of praising her legs,
and leaving her colleagues as obscure as she found them.

What is revealing about this three-ring performance is that it
followed closely upon personal heartbreak. In January 1944 Clare's
only child, Ann, died in a freak car accident, being bounced out of
the passenger seat against a tree while driving with a sorority sister
from Stanford—an accident in which *everything* had to go wrong for
death to occur—and a few years later, Clare was to write a scorch-
ing account of just how much this hurt. It is generally believed that
she quit politics almost immediately after the tragedy: but she
didn't, she ran again in her most pugnacious vein. In fact, "GI Jim"
would have been around her daughter's age. Ann would have been
twenty on her next birthday. Although the long-range effect of
Ann's death was to drive Clare into temporary retirement, far away
from the flashbulbs and wisecracks, its immediate effect was to
drive her the other way, into ever more flamboyant activity, and
more bellicose politics. The hairy reelection drive of '44 and the
Italian Carnival were her response to grief; one must fight, one must

live. Clare was often at her most outrageous when she was hurting all over.

These were the reflexes that had propelled her so far, and for a while they free-wheeled gaudily before coming to rest. It wasn't just the death of Ann that slowed her down in the end, but a series of personal blows that she could only hide for so long, like a game prizefighter—the death of her mother, the cooling of Harry, and several suicides of friends. Anyway, she quit Washington at the end of 1946, walking with steady steps out of her cherished lime-light. The dreaded Luce takeover had not occurred. She had not played Evita. Perhaps it had never entered her mind.

Because of the time lag, one might be tempted to suppose that the heartbreak over Ann was an afterthought. But if so, it is an af-terthought that has been sustained a mighty long time. When she visits Ann's grave in South Carolina, she still breaks down. And when she talks about her, there is a quality of regret that even her mother and brother do not evoke. After all, David and Ann, Sr., lived out their lives, and their fates now seem inevitable, for what-ever comfort that's worth, and thoroughly arrived at. Ann just walked out the door, one feels. What did one say to her last? Was it nice or other? How unfair not to be warned. Ann is an absence, a lost opportunity.

The ineffable Ms. Lawrenson describes in her *Esquire* article a birthday party for Ann at Ridgefield, where the child was fobbed off with a worthless present and then royally ignored. How Lawrenson knows what value a particular present might have for a particular person, I don't know. (For Ann's last Christmas, Harry had his people hunting high and low for the perfect present, which turned out to be a pair of $300 earrings, so Ann wasn't always slighted.) But the scene is what every parent who has lost a child must dread, whether it has happened or not—but it's usually hap-pened, all right.

Imagining the worst, as is my wont, I tried to guess the impact of a scene stealer like Clare on a teen-ager. Her dinner table per-formances might be just the thing to grate on someone at that age, for whom authenticity is all, and to whom the idea of a public self and a private self seems a particularly repellent twist on growing up. Actors' children seem to despise their parents with some special force, and maybe politicians' do too: not because they get too little attention, but because the attention they do get can be turned off so brutally, or else faked, in the presence of an audience. Five minutes of unholy fuss over the child, and then, get lost.

Remembering my own tour as surrogate young person, I would guess perhaps that a little of this happened, but if so it was probably more irritating than traumatic. Most witnesses by defini-tion only saw Ann and Clare in public, and you can't really win with an adolescent in public: attention, lack of attention, it all hurts. A party of grown-ups puts you down, while a party of kids is an insult. Bored or ignored, even quite normal adolescents manage to look as if their parents beat them secretly. If Clare and Ann had a precisely average mother-daughter relationship, there would still be something to regret. Or so I felt upon reading Lawrenson's thoughtful piece, championing the underdog child who could no longer feel the good of it, and wounding the living.*

With no more information to go on as yet, I still figured that if Clare was half as alertly sympathetic with Ann as she is with chil-dren now, then Ann got pretty good value—when she had Clare at all. The real problem would not have been such everyman scenes as Lawrenson witnessed but sheer physical absence. It was no easier then than it is now to build a career and be even a half-time mother: and Clare was building about seven careers. Although as I've dis-covered, Clare shuttled about furiously to close the gap, she does admit her regret at not seeing more of Ann, especially during the war correspondent period.

Then, too, there was the notoriety effect. Ann's adolescence coincided with Clare's firework years, the plays, the first congres-sional heroics, flashbulbs everywhere. *I see your mother got in the paper again.* Only a child with a rhino hide can enjoy a public parent. And however much Clare made it up to her in private, Ann had to share her mother with the world in a most flamboyant form.

To counteract this, Clare conscientiously did not drag her daughter into the limelight, though she would have made a most attractive ornament, bright and pretty and "nice"-looking: not fat or furtive, like a spoiled, neglected, celebrity brat. Ann looked as if she came from a normal American family, which is quite a feat for a superstar's daughter, whoever gets the credit for it.

One of Clare's unexpected gifts is keeping in touch with unex-pected people (she doesn't, in my experience, answer letters, but fires off her own out of the blue, or phones up impulsively). Per-haps Norman Ross is not so unexpected: he did propose to Ann the

---

* Helen Lawrenson, "The Woman," *Esquire*, August, 1974. Lawrenson herself may have felt this was a bit much. At least, I couldn't find the episode anywhere in her collection *Stranger at the Party* (NY, Random House, 1975.) A little late in the day to help.

night before she died, and was provisionally accepted. But what is perhaps unusual about his case is that Clare barely knew him before that, but has become fast friends with him ever since.

Anyway, Ross reports that Ann "loved and admired her mother—adored her really," but that she somehow gave the impression that she could have used a more average life at times. At any rate, she peeled potatoes and slid down banisters at the Rosses' with the zest of someone who has been denied these things.

When the time came for Norman to meet the formidable Luces, Ann was anxious that he make a good impression on her parents. "Be sure to look my father straight in the eye when you talk to him. He hates people who don't do that." (If only someone had told *me* that. It could have turned everything around.) It's a welcome slap of reality, after the greasepaint we've been wading through, to find Ann calling her stepfather "Father." But it's been amply confirmed by others that she meant it. She liked Harry enormously, as their brief correspondence verifies. As for Harry's own feelings: the night of Ann's funeral, Mr. Ross and a fellow pallbearer named Walton Wickett found him picking at a book in a restaurant and wondering whether he shouldn't have skipped publishing altogether and joined the ministry like his father. Either that or service in World War II . . . Later, as we shall see, he asked to be buried next to Ann and Clare at Mepkin.

And as for Clare, perhaps her feelings can be dimly divined from a letter she wrote Ann four years earlier—I have to guess four years because the letter is simply datelined "Friday." As I say, Clare's mind does not run to dates. But she was apparently sailing off to keep her appointment with Europe in the spring of 1940. I print it in full because it conveys so much: her guilt over leaving Ann one more time; her eagerness to make it up to her, all in one go; the trouble she took to ask and report the right things in the right tone of voice. If a daughter is left alone on the dock, what would she like to hear? Regret and light-heartedness mingled; reminders that life goes on in its funny, exasperating way; a sense that separation is just a silly technicality anyway. No one letter can sum up a whole relationship, but this is a start.

> Annie my darling—You were a grand little trouper about my going and I really loved you better at the moment, for the swell way you took it, more than I ever did perhaps before! I hated to go off without you, but I was so physically and mentally exhausted that I did not have the courage to renounce the trip once it was definitely decided upon.

Naturally, I'm palpitating to find out what *you* think of the house, how you liked your room (if it was ready!), does the pool, the court, etc. "work," and anything else you may feel about the place. So write me at once, if you have not already done so.

The trip has been very, very quiet. There are very few people aboard. The ship will carry 1200—only 320 are on it, either because the others have become too poor or are afraid of a sudden outbreak of war. It's a handsome ship—rather better than the Queen Mary, especially the food! But the movies they have on board are sumpin orful. (Don't *ever* go to see the Gracie Allen Murder Case, by the way!) There's nobody to play ping-pong with, either, which is sad. I *do* miss you and Dad quite a lot and I suspect I shall miss you a lot more when I'm all rested up and slept out!

Darling, thank you for your wire and your last round of posies while I was in the hospital. Such courtesies—such gentle thoughts are what makes life gay and pleasant! You are often very adept at them.

Listen, there's a very high sea on now, and the cabin is groaning and squealing and cracking and wailing in every joint, and as we roll from one side to the other, the curtains, my dresses on hooks stand away at right angles from the wall, I find my thoughts more occupied with what crashes of glass or furniture will mark the end of each heave-to, than with this letter, so perhaps I'd better stop until the sea is a bit calmer. . . . You and Kit would both be feeling *very* badly, if you were here! (Did I tell you, Kit was going to have another baby, and then she got a bit careless about her health, and lost it? Isn't that too bad?) (Whoops—there goes a flower vase and one with flowers in it from Greenwich, too!) Oh, well, I've rung for Bertha (my new maid) to straighten it out, so I might as well go on with this letter until she comes. Incidentally the difference between store flowers and your own garden flowers seems to be that store flowers are all flowers and no leaves, and your own are all leaves, and few flowers. Wonder why?

No, it's impossible to write: I keep lurching from side to side like a jitterbug dancer, and the pencils, and even the photo of you on the table beside me (I've changed it to a snap of you doing a "Hula") keep travelling so! So—until tomorrow, my tall, beautiful, kind little angel. (I am just *dying* for a letter from you!)

Now here it is, tomorrow, and the ship is still as prankish as ever! But the cabin seems more used to it somehow, and is not making such a yammer in every joint. So I will go in a bit.

Hdya like the new clothes? Do you look adorable in that little frilled bathing suit, or didn't you like it? Is the green tea gown with the frills flattering or isn't it? Please send me lots of news in your first letter. Also, how's Patsy's house, mother and Pa! How's Cassie? Have you played Bezique with the old man? Did you go to the wonderful

World's Fair? And so on and so on. You'd think perhaps that I'd be the one with the news, seeing as how I'm travelling to Europe on a big boat, but I've spent so much time sleeping in my state room, and seen no one "new" and nothing but yards of water, I haven't much to tell. I've got a nice new maid—not nearly as good as Mary tho'—who talks too much when I'm trying to read or write (breakers ahead!) and who slammed her fingers in a door the second day out, so she can't pack so well, poor thing, and I've got too much luggage as usual and that's all the news I have.

I send you millions, BUT millions of kisses my sweetheart. Your Mother.

At the bottom of the fifth and last page, Clare draws a pocket cartoon of a lady weeping out of a porthole in the general direction of Harry Luce (not a bad drawing at all) and "you" (not drawn). I find the letter especially touching because the new house with the court and the swimming pool has to be the Ridgefield house where I gamboled in 1949. I can see now why she was so willing to plant another teen-ager by the pool.

Anyway, the person she wrote to with all that melancholy gusto was suddenly gone, the one child she'd been able to have, snuffed out by a ridiculous accident—it must have been too much even for Clare's immaculate composure. Mr. Ross remembers holding up his hand to ward a *Life* camera out of her face at the funeral, to keep at least her grief private. Remember he had only just met her, and already he was seeing a woman few people, if any, had ever seen before: a Clare without defenses. He says simply that she seemed much more vulnerable than her legend. If she hadn't been before, she was now.

Meanwhile, back in the land of make-believe; not too long before Ann died, a little book came out called *Au Clare de Luce*, by one Faye Henle, which sums up the state of Clare criticism at the time, and would be grounds, in my opinion, for anyone to leave public life in mild despair. After years of competing with men on their own terms, Clare gets treated to this kind of talk. "There was a period of slim hands flashing, well-modelled shoulders in animated action" is apparently what happened when one met Clare in those days. Before delivering the globaloney speech she gave "a premonitory rake with her claws," the start of an extraordinary physical performance. "In the first place, the lady looked like a pussycat, a sleepy, ineffably confident pussycat, ever so lightly lashing a mischievous plume." And on.

The author wouldn't have dared say that about William Pitt. But that's how the women wrote about the woman, and it's enough to make anyone wonder, "What's the use?" Whatever Clare had learned about timing and irony was briskly transferred to the cat box. The author refers throughout to Clare's "brilliance," but what use is such brilliance as this? Eyes glittering, claws raking—I would take my own cat's maiden speech more seriously.

And Clare's whole career is diminished to this scale throughout the book. "Surgery for the second time had changed the life of a Boothe," Henle announces, in one of my favorite lines. Clare, it seems, was inordinately lucky (just when she needed it—an appendectomy!), which already makes her sound like a creature from the Black Lagoon. Only witchcraft or fiendish calculation could account for such a beautiful, successful creature, even in this century. Exorcise the cat before she gets Henry Wallace!

The final sign of the lady monster is, as we know, a preternatural coldness. She may set men on fire, even old Harry Luce, but her own heart is an ice cube. Henle can barely get through a chapter without reminding us of this. Even when she grudgingly admits that Clare was well known for her unusual acts of kindness, she adds that somehow nobody could ever associate these with warmth. How's that? Did the victims feel an icy chill as Madam handed over the goods? Clare de la Luce, cold as charity, bright as the moon.

As I say, this stuff must be hard to take, not because it's malicious—in fact, the tone is frequently fawning, as if she might want to use Clare again—but because it's so incorrigibly silly. Henle even has Clare emerging from the Pacific jungles immaculately gowned and deliciously perfumed. ("I wasn't. I was dirty and smelly and needed a bath.") With every allowance for hack's license, this is a dismal way for one woman to be writing about another. After so many years of trailblazing, Clare could still count on finding a female hired gun at the end of the tunnel, eager to do a man's job.

In fact, all her critics seemed to be women, as if men were ineligible. Another assassination attempt was made in *The New Yorker* in the early forties by one Margaret Case Harriman (no relation to the Margaret Case skewered in *Europe in the Spring*), another old *Vanity Fair* hand. It was called "The Candor Kid," but I had read so much Clare criticism by the time I got to it that I was beginning to turn a little green myself, so I decided to pass it up. When I mentioned the old profile to Clare, her only surviving complaint was that the author had her surreptitiously strewing crumbs on the ground at Mepkin so the birds would land there and be literal sitting ducks. "That would be awful, that would be cheating," she says, still angry.

If we add this to our Lawrenson and our Henle we have the basic portrait of a witch: she lies about her origins, is cold, feline, and preternaturally lucky, and over and above everything she cheats. Depressing news to hear about oneself. Even though Henle's book could be read as a campaign document, these can hurt too.

However, with so much real sorrow going around, I imagine the book slid off Clare harmlessly enough. It might have interested her to read about how lucky the Boothe women were supposed to be, or how totally lacking in feeling, but she had more on her mind than that. The furious campaign of 1944 and the GI Jim furor have to be seen in the light from Ann's funeral. Hyperactivity is one solution to grief, and Clare seemed to be taking it out on everyone. Like a maddened gardener ripping at weeds, she wanted to eliminate evil everywhere at once. But things run down after a while. Roosevelt dies; Clare's monomania, the war, ends at last; all the targets, in Fitzgerald's phrase, are down. In 1946, she chooses not to run for anything ever again.

She did not snivel or break down so's you'd notice. She wrote some confessional pieces for *McCall's*,* about the secular dead ends she had wandered down, and the wasteland of all those clever careers she now saw strewn around her. But it was a lament for a generation, and a point of view, and not just a private loss of nerve. And it went deeper than politics, as what does not?

That was the public face. Privately she may have shown a little more. She wrote a number of letters to good old Bernie Baruch, very circumspect, at least as they appear in Baruch's possibly expurgated correspondence in the Princeton University Library, but perhaps cries for help. She also wrote a quite hysterical letter about the evil nature of men to her old friend Lawrenson, which Lawrenson sees fit to hint at somewhat luridly in her, as I say, curious essay. I leave it to her.

Baruch, on the other hand, told no tales. So we bid farewell to that garrulous enigma. Clare and Harry had by chance built their Mepkin estate (or rather had Edward Durrell Stone build it for

---

* Clare Boothe Luce, "The Real Reason," *McCall's Magazine*, February, March, April, 1947.

them) in the vicinity of Baruch's place. Since Luce himself did not care for Baruch in the slightest, I find myself dimly reminded of Clare's mother and her friend Joseph Jacobs. Mrs. Boothe, as you recall, had married her respectable Protestant, Dr. Austin, as Clare did hers. But Jacobs continued to come round for pinochle anyway. And so it went, on a somewhat ritzier level, with Clare and Bernie. He was something solid in her life and she was damned if she was going to let go of it. (Of Jews in general she says, "It's nice to have a chosen people that really worked out.")

It had been an amazing span of years from 1929, when she walked away from Brokaw to 1946, when she walked away from public life. Editor, playwright, newshen (as they were then called), author, congresswoman, fashion plate—it's hard to think what more she could have done without seeming ostentatious.

I thought of Clare when I first heard the Cole Porter song "Why don't we try staying home?" ("we've done everything else twice"). And staying home, of course, is where I found her, and where we came in. But I gather home itself had changed in the last few years.

Irwin Shaw, who visited the Luces at Mepkin, South Carolina, as a guest of Helen Lawrenson's in the late thirties, assures me that Clare "ran" Harry completely back then. This was certainly not so by the time I met them in '49, except in the superficial sense in which women are often said to dominate their husbands, by out-talking them (this relationship was, of course, a commonplace in American families, and a staple of cartoons, soaps, etc. Even by that fatuous standard, the Luces seemed to me abnormally equal).

Shaw also remembers the jaunty young Clare showing him how to wring a bird's neck and daring him, as a city boy, to do like-wise. On the same principle, she got him to ride a somewhat met-tlesome horse (which he did with ease, having ridden in Prospect Park as a kid). It went without saying that Clare was also a good shot. By what seemed like dint of will, she was good at just about everything.

As an old football player, Shaw found this tomboy stuff exhil-arating, not depressing as some might; and it does bring to mind pictures of young Clare and David racing up rain barrels, diving off haylofts, testing each other's courage. Shaw still emphasizes the playfulness rather than the hardness, the girl who wants to play with the boys on even terms, physically and mentally.

But again, none of this horseplay would have been imaginable with the Clare I met ten years later. She was still quite sporting, teaching me how to serve a tennis ball with my stiff-legged brace and giving me swimming tips, but gently. There was no neck-wringing about it. In fact I would never have guessed, even from her whimsical jigsaw puzzling, that I was dealing with one of the great competitive dynamos of our time. Something had changed.

# CHAPTER SIX

# *The View from the Bunkhouse, 1949–77*

So this was the Clare I met in 1949. She had already fallen off her horse and seen the light of Christianity, so I never knew Clare I, the famous pagan. Many people didn't notice the difference, partly because there wasn't a trace of sackcloth about her and partly because she had to go and get converted by Fulton Sheen, official priest to the celebrities. Sheen, I later learned, was a technicality: she had originally applied to a simple Polish priest, who passed her on like a hot potato to the brainy monsignor. Catholicism spoke to her because her Bavarian mother still carried traces of it, and she wanted something like that: peasant-sturdy, not pompous-ceremonial. Still, one is not to suppose a complete change of character. She did say, in deference to her Act, that she wanted a confessor "who had talked with kings and emperors."

But the religious impulse was quite solid and unflashy. After some invigorating jousting with Sheen, she moved on to plainer fare, and there was no further prattle about kings and emperors. As recounted already, she didn't see Uncle Fultie once the whole time I was with her, or indeed any other stars of stage, screen, or altar. She did discuss theology with my father, Frank Sheed, whose most congenial habitat was the street corner platform where for years he tangled happily with drunks and rationalists and all the flotsam of big cities. Without exposing that good man, I would have to say that his dinner jacket was a shade more disreputable than mine, owing to his habit of stuffing it into shopping bags, while over his regular clothes it might be best to draw a veil (he can have one of mine). Any glamour Frank exuded was not of this world. You did not talk religion to him unless you were serious enough to break a sweat.

After taking a brilliant law degree at Sydney University, Frank had abruptly abandoned all that ("When I realized that some law-yers were paid more than others, I knew that there was no justice") to take up the Catholic Church as a sort of legal brief—and if there *were* any justice, he'd have received a fee for it like unto Clarence Darrow's. I have never met a nimbler arguer, though Clare bounced along with him very well. (When he asked how she was making out with Aquinas' *Summa Theologica*, she confessed that "one swallow does not make a summa.")

Anyway, Frank's rumpled, unconcerned presence in Clare's living room might have surprised Clare's ever-faithful critics who assumed that her conversion was just another chic move by the icy blonde. To Frank Sheed, this was just another house.

Now, in 1950, that I knew Clare personally, I watched her public self acting out its appointed drama in a whole new way, learning how much of it was in the eye of the beholder, like the trompe l'oeil in *Margin for Error*, where the audience makes up what it's seeing, and how much was the person I knew, only blown up so you can see the pores.

Since the only thing she was visibly doing in the early fifties was being Catholic, the Clareophobes and -ophiles had to make what they could of that. The Bishop Sheen connection was usually good for a laugh (he showed little angels on his TV show, for pete sake), but nobody really minded Sheen. He was a decent man in a childish period who'd gone a teensy bit too far. But Cardinal Spell-man was something else. Although Clare doesn't even make the index of Robert Gannon's exhaustive biography of Spellman, and he certainly wasn't a houseguest, their glancing friendship had symbolic significance. In those days Spellman was busily building himself up, like a snowman, into a liberal nemesis by such moves as denouncing Eleanor Roosevelt, personally breaking a gravedig-gers' strike, and later honoring Joe McCarthy at table. Clare's rela-tionship with him was largely pastoral and social, stemming from her marriage situation vis-à-vis the Church, but given their political track records few people believed this, because few people thought of Spellman as a priest at all.

He is worth dwelling on for a moment because he represented the side of the Church Clare had entered—Clare not knowing that the Church had sides and that this was *not* the tradesman's entrance.

Actually, Spellie, or his Remnants, as we guttersnipes called His Eminence Francis J. Spellman, was rumored to be an affable fellow in private, who once delivered the endearing line, "Frankly, I prefer the Vargas girl to the Venus de Milo," but he really was quite the bogeyman in public. Besides looking like a cartoon in *Krokodil,* he seemed, all too often, to act like one, running his diocese like the late Mayor Daley's Chicago, with a touch of Cosimo de' Medici thrown in. The businessman/priest has always cut a satiric figure, however heaven-oriented his business might be. Building schools and hospitals is still building, which means a buzz of contractors and realtors, plus a special attention to those wealthy souls who congregate in such pest-holes as golf clubs and expensive restaurants. A prince of the Church puts his soul at risk with every cornerstone.

Spellman was twice-cursed, because even his great virtue, his unpretentiousness, was held against him. The plumb ordinariness that seemed so attractive in Chesterton's Father Brown looked like well-fed mediocrity in Spellman because of the company he kept. If he was a bad friend for Clare in some eyes, people like Clare were bad friends for him, the simple priest of the people. Yet what was Spellman to do? He was sitting on a gold mine, the richest diocese in the world, and it was his spiritual duty to turn it to account. ("Spiritual" may sound cynical in that context. Yet for every priest who actually enjoys the lugubrious company of the rich, there must be at least two who would give their eyeteeth to retire to a mountain cave before they have to face another fat cat. Schools, churches, hospitals come at a wicked price in ulcers and boredom and teeth-gritting patience.)

Spellman, behind the mongol mask, might have been enjoying himself for all one knew—although he also looked, like many bishops, as if his feet hurt all the time. There were moments of peevish aggression, such as the Eleanor Roosevelt incident (he called some remarks of hers "unworthy of an American mother," then made peace with her over tea at Hyde Park), that suggest either unhappiness or well-earned indigestion. One day he stalked off a platform where my father was speaking because, having dozed through the body of the lecture, he awoke to some line that apparently annoyed him. He wouldn't speak to my father for a year, and then just as mysteriously forgave him.

If Spellman was a bad friend, in those same eyes, for Clare in the forties, he became a worse one later, as his caged combativeness made him virtually the official chaplain to the cold war. By then his whole world was roaring down the drain. His power base was crumbling; those spanking new churches were half-empty, and his deluxe seminary at Dunwoodie was a ghost town; and any day his teachers were going to start asking for money. It's a lot to ask of a man, if you throw in *Baby Doll** as well. But none of this was in sight when Clare Luce first entered his little gold rush kingdom in the 1940s.

One problem that did come rippling down from the top right away was the general presumption that Mrs. Luce's income and fame bracket had entitled her to go on living with a divorced man with the Church's approval. It is a mark of Spellman's stoical delicacy that he never corrected this misapprehension. In this, he probably did more overall harm than good, reinforcing the impression of a double standard for rich and poor, but his treatment of the matter was priestly (i.e., "To hell with public opinion") and it won him Clare's friendship, as stoical silence usually does. If she wanted the truth about herself and Harry to come out, that was her business.

Now that Harry is dead, and the issue has cooled a bit, she presumably doesn't mind the truth coming out, which was what I should have guessed had I been paying attention that summer: namely, that she and Harry had not lived together connubially for some time before the conversion. Harry's famous conscience made it impossible for him to conduct two affairs at once, so as soon as someone, anyone, else came along, that was that. Whoever came along, I deduce, did so after about five years. If so, it suggests that their professional partnership got stronger as the chemistry got weaker. This physical estrangement was one of the several blows that drove Clare toward Catholicism, a move that Presbyterian Harry, perhaps relieved, encouraged warmly.

Spellman, for all his famous rigidity, was enormously sympa-

---

* *Baby Doll* and *The Moon Is Blue,* two excessively silly movies even by fifties standards, were especial torments to his eminence: the latter for its tinny Broadway sophistication, the former for its embryonic decadence. Once again, he preferred the Vargas girl.

thetic, and even favored their staying together so long as the companionship side of their marriage held up and was fruitful to them. This was grounds enough for Clare's friendship—but unfortunately, it was invisible, and all the public could see was two cold warriors clanking glasses.

Clare always felt a kinship for people like Spellman and Herbert Hoover who allowed themselves to be vilified beyond their merits. In Spellman's case, she also understood his odd function in life better than most of his flock. To her the disposition of money was part of the world's work, and nothing to get exercised about, and Spellman had to seem at least a better man than most of the tycoons she was used to. The central question of whether the Church should be in the money market at all was understandably muted in the better pulpits, and a rich convert could easily have missed it altogether. In fact, such a one might even have been encouraged to stay as rich as you are, even by relatively humble prelates, wrestling with mortgages they never asked for.

It would have been against nature for Clare not to go right to the top of anything: it would have been cowardice. But the top of a virtuous organization should have been safe enough. (Assuredly she would have been hustled even more by the second stringers, and would have seemed like the ultimate hot dog if she'd played missionary to the poor.) But unfortunately there has always been a counterculture in the Catholic Church, for whom poverty is *the* sign of faith, the password, and inevitably it attracts its share of bright young people, who are just at the age to form lifelong prejudices. Clare struck their vision like a Bonwit Teller Christmas ad. However muted, she gave comfort to their fat parents. Thus, without knowing it, Clare had stirred up a fresh bloc of hecklers, who, whatever compromises they might later make themselves, would never soften an inch toward *her* compromises.

A more clouded issue, one that brought her both friends and more critics, was anticommunism. She might reasonably have supposed that on this score at least she would receive no grief at all from her coreligionists. Catholics had overwhelmingly good reason to be anti-Communist. For one thing, as is often forgotten, communism had started the fight. The Vatican notoriously will bargain with just about anybody to protect its people; but Russian and Chinese Christians were not given the choice. They were persecuted without benefit of bargaining, on a scale that the secular mind never seemed to grasp or care about. (The Alger Hiss type didn't even look as if it cared—the kind of historical grace note that sometimes gets lost.)

Congresswoman Luce was of course on record as having opposed the iron curtain while it was still going up. But she couldn't have bargained on the raggletail mob of anti-Communists who joined her now, all itching to exploit the chip on Catholic *and* nativist shoulders (the nativists* were really sore about things like zoning boards and do-good taxing, but it all came under the heading of *communism* to them).

There were different goodies under the tree for different people. For a Spellman, anticommunism rallied his flock into a Church militant and gave a fighting edge to their faith, while it also made him seem nationally important, a quasi-statesman; for Joe McCarthy, it gave a classic American showman a chance to do his stuff, and eventually to make a mockery of the whole cause; for "the Luces," it was a chance to fulfill a lifelong dream of a global America, wielding a power and vitality like unto their own, in the cause of Western Christian civilization. Clare's friend Senator Arthur Vandenberg had told Harry Truman, "You've got to scare hell out of them," in order to get Americans involved in the outside world at all. In other words, you cannot have a Marshall Plan without a cold war; you cannot do good without an enemy to do it against.

Both Clare and Harry felt that isolationism would stunt America's growth and choke off its manifest destiny, which Harry had made his own, and they were willing to do whatever amount of saber-rattling would prevent this. But for them it had to be good clean saber-rattling, not the back-alley switch-blade stuff McCarthy went in for. Unfortunately, since most Americans can see only two of everything, us and them, Left and Right, all the anti-Communists found themselves herded into the same tent, like so many liberals. It was in vain for *Time* to attack Joe McCarthy as a vulgarian; Spellman gave Joe a memorial dinner, to bolster his own constituency; Fulton Sheen and Spellman went to Australia together to review the Pax Americana, as a sort of benign Cohn and Schine, and Clare was Sheen's convert. Around and around went the web, saints and knaves all weaving together.

McCarthy gave the Right a bad name, in which the Luces

---

* A Catholic woman I know bought into a local right-wing bookstore only to find that half the produce was rabidly anti-papist.

willy-nilly received their share. But he also gave it protection in the Mafia style. This had nothing to do with specific witch-hunts. It has often been said that Joe never came up with any real Communists, but it can be seriously debated whether he needed to. The chief object of the game was simply to neutralize the American Left and to keep it from mounting sustained attacks on such institutions as NATO and SEATO and our overseas military investment, or on the business structure at home that complements these: all Luce's babies. And in this respect, McCarthyism was a smashing success, with or without victims, with or without Joe himself.

For Luce to become a moderate, a mighty displacement had to occur, as with a large man on an elevator; and this was taken care of by the goon squad. By calling George Marshall a traitor and Dean Acheson "the Red Dean of Washington" the McCarthy gang moved the Left so far to the center that you could barely call it a Left at all. One spent so much time denying that one was a Communist or even a Socialist or a disarmer or a troop-withdrawer that the statement one finally felt free to make was scrupulously emasculated. This was the era that spawned liberals like Dean Rusk and Walt Rostow and John F. Kennedy (who, as we know, took sick leave when McCarthy was censured), colder-than-thou warriors against the veriest hint of communism.

Insofar as the Luce interventionist Right considered this a tolerable climate (it certainly made the Pax Americana hum), they can be said to have profited from McCarthyism, as a southern aristocrat profits from a redneck sheriff. With Clare, this tenuous link further alienated her from the young Catholic Left, which was having its own troubles. We were damned if we were going to be called Communists by anybody. But McCarthyism had given so many blunt weapons to the know-nothings that we spent desperate evenings distinguishing among shades of pink and agreeing finally to denounce McCarthy's "methods," as if McCarthy were anything *but* methods and as if his methods were not the sole reason for our having to argue like this in the first place.

So outside of Dorothy Day's radical pacifism, which was conveniently easy to label as crackpot (Dorothy let all her followers talk at once, so it certainly had that side), and the gentlemanly thrusts of *Commonweal*, there was no leftish voice in Clare's new Church worth worrying about or arguing with. To make up for the public silence, Catholic liberals were vociferously sarcastic among themselves and in private, and the whole Catholic anti-Communist apparatus got it in the neck indiscriminately, whether Buckley or

Spellman or Luce. They might have learned their precision in accusation from Joe McCarthy himself.

I felt briefly abandoned by my hostess. Clare's anticommunism had been, as I absorbed it with half an ear, specifically anti-Stalinist: it had to do with the rape of Eastern Europe, with the relatives of émigrés waiting for news, with pain-in-your-knees Christianity—with all of which the Catholic Left sympathized fully. This anti-Stalinism had nothing to do with one's feeling about capitalism *per se:* you could love the latter to distraction or despise it —it was simply a separate subject. I had hoped that Clare of all people would make these distinctions now, but I guess it was sociologically impossible. Fulton Sheen would talk in his spiffy bishop's regalia of Russia as "the cross without Christ," and of us the other way around, but it was just talk: his robes *were* the message so Clare didn't have a chance. If she talked about Eastern Europe, it was just the rich Luces playing politics, building spheres of influence, making the world safe for John Foster Dulles. Whatever her private pain, she was too well fixed to talk about sacrifice.

Whether, to prove a point, Clare could have given up *her* regalia, any part of her servants and her high style, which she had fought for so hard, is an abstract question that probably never got asked within earshot. The loss would have been excruciating, but the call to greatness irresistible. Maybe in the late forties, for a little while . . . however, as I say, nobody who was anybody suggested it. It would have been considered as mad then as it would be today. The Church had wound itself up tight in the American flag, which at the time suspiciously resembled a cash register on a field of gold bars. If Russia was bad, then money must be very good indeed, practically beatific. Fund-raising and godless Communism were so jumbled together in sermons that the pulpit seemed half auctioneer's block, half patriotic rally: a bully pulpit indeed. Clare had joined the Church at the height of its Rotund Feline period, and was taken unwittingly as a minor symbol of it by the Young Turks of the day.

The sheer size of the Catholic Left was not fully revealed until it began burning draft cards and carrying on. The kids were at last proclaiming the values they had learned quietly at home. But in the fifties, we were as silent as the next fellow, and if someone like Clare gave an occasional "America the Perfect" speech, she had every reason to believe that Catholics were behind her to a man. The adulation she did receive was blinding and deafening, from college platform to Communion breakfast: and in those days, the

Catholic ghetto was a Kingdom you could ride around in forever and never reach the edge. It was also, on the other side of the boundary, the only religion liberals felt free to sneer at. Their only idea of a good Catholic was a secular humanist like Father George B. Ford—as if secular humanism were the divine truth to which all religions must grope, more or less successfully. So Clare was walled in with her new friends. Many valuable dialogues were canceled in the fifties, but the one I personally missed was the one between Clare Luce and the Catholic Left—a chance for the old playwright to bounce her lines off something new. I hated to watch that intelligence wasting itself on simpering college presidents. I was afraid she wasn't getting enough competition.

However, you either mix with the rich or you don't: bull sessions with them are rare. In those days, nobody went around demanding confrontations, and the Luces seemed to reign from a distant planet, infinitely inaccessible. My father, who'll try anything in this line, had Dorothy Day and Clare to lunch together one day, but no sparks flew. Clare did admire Day, and didn't give a fig about her politics, but Day, I imagine, considered Clare a royal waste of time. "I know you think it's Christian to forgive Hitler," my father once said to Dorothy, "but what about the president of General Motors?" So the meeting was doomed. The Left wouldn't have given Clare a chance if she'd gone down on her knees. Not in those clothes, anyway.

From where I sat, I was to note that, as the fifties rolled into the sixties, the public Clare seemed to drift not so much further right, which was perfectly natural, as out of range. Her voice seemed to come from some far-off boardroom rather than next to my elbow. It was as if the restricted company Clare kept was getting to her at last. My parents and other spies reported the same mix of dinner guests: either smart and famous, or rich and dull. Since the latter outnumber the former on Millionaires' Row, I feared the worst. And in her occasional essays, she seemed to me to be talking in a closed room to the same old dinner party.

My father reports to me that he once told Clare that she didn't know enough nobodies, and she answered, "But are they interesting?" As usual, half funny and half not.

She wrote a play in 1951 about St. Maria Goretti, the little Italian girl who died defending her honor, and it got as far as Boston, starring Margaret O'Brien (!) and Eddie Dowling. Clare was strongly moved by the subject, though in one of her chronic oblique moments, she said, "I guess at twelve I would have said 'no' too." She should have trusted that mood, she worked better in it (my father used to say, "Saint is just another word for an Italian virgin," and he was a theologian), but she wasn't going to go back to her wise-guy phase for anybody. The play got no farther than Boston, but there is no more sincere test of one's faith than to write a flop for it, and she may have felt as if she'd discharged a duty.

Anyway, she emerged from retirement in the 1950s, which signaled that her battle against publicity was either lost or won: at any rate, over. Perhaps she felt she had the upper hand on it now and could face the light without losing her soul. As Thomas Merton seems also to have discovered in his last years, it is possible to be a Catholic and a cutup at the same time. If Clare had temporarily come to the end of the line as a spiritual seeker, she might have been finding seclusion a barren business anyway. As a far-flung friend, I was not really sorry. Her mid-life retreat had been invaluable, but activity was her essence. You can't force a contemplative vocation beyond a point, and the only question was whether she could activate her contemplation and put it to use: i.e., would she resume the old flash, or would she do something more solid?

From the sidelines, it looked like a bit of both. After running for the Senate in 1952, and getting soundly whomped, she wisely pulled out of electoral politics. The slow squirreling away of delegates and IOU's and voting blocs was not for her anymore. She got sandbagged at the State Convention because her infighting was rusty. John Lodge, whose support she had reason to count on, swiped the nomination himself. Despite an Arrow collar face and mind if ever I saw one (he still stands out gleaming among the meatballs of Summer 1949), Lodge was just smart enough for that. Clare rallied with one of her best fight quotes, "I will lay me down and bleed awhile / then I'll rise and fight with you again" (Dryden), but for once she didn't do it.

Instead, in 1953, she became Ambassador to Italy (the first woman, naturally, to hold such an important post), where she attracted no more than the inevitable number of garish headlines for the next four years. It's hard to tell from the outside how well any ambassador is doing, so for now I'll stick to the generalities that occurred to a slack-jawed youth of the period.

Clare is to the limelight what certain actors are to the camera: they love each other on a level almost below consciousness, and can find each other in a London fog. But the earlier Clare would have caused ten times more fuss in Italy than the later model. At the beginning of her hitch, she was accused of meddling in Italian politics (by suggesting which vote would please the Signora most in the current election), and at the end she accused the ceiling of trying to poison her, but in between she made only such news as is proper to an ambassador in the land of the paparazzi and the leak.

A celebrity ambassador can draw more attention than a diplomat should, but she can also publicize certain national interests better than a faceless functionary. Clare seems to have got this just about right and she made a noise only about the few things that mattered. In fact, she did so well that people began to say it was really Harry pulling the strings: just as it was George S. Kaufman who wrote *The Women*, and somebody else who edited *Vanity Fair*. None of this quiet competence, of course, had the slightest effect on her hardcore detractors, who believed that she always goes looking for the press and never the other way around, just as *she* pursued Harry, and that if she isn't in the paper every day it's because she can't always get its attention.

As far as politics proper were concerned, Clare's Italian image was neutral if not benign. Just as her boss Eisenhower seemed to have no ideology whatever, nor even the makings of an ideology, so Clare in the fifties seemed to be somewhere in the middle of the consensus—if one bears in mind that the center was now on the right. Our bipartisan foreign policy, the end product of the McCarthy adventure, had herded everyone into this small area, and for once Clare's opinions were lost in the crowd. In Italy, *any* ambassador would have backed the Christian Democrats, and done what he could for Italian claims to Trieste: according to Eisenhower's own memoirs, Clare simply did both (especially Trieste) better than most.

She had gone to Rome, as she had to Washington, with the idea that you were supposed to *do* something, else why waste public time and money? One of the embarrassments about Clare is that she won't just take an honorific job, and leave it at that. Who knows what cables worked and what didn't? Many Italians loved her (she still gets the hand-kissing mail to prove it) and perhaps they will make her a saint in due time. Santa Chiara of Trieste, patron of the Via Magna, or Big Way.

Trieste was one of those exasperating cases, like the North of Ireland, where two sides have at least plausible claims. The welter of treaties signed in this century allotted Trieste to both Italy *and* Yugoslavia. The latter, feeling its oats under Tito, was pushing very hard for this Mediterranean plum: Clare pushed back on behalf of the Italians. What brand of carrots she used or whether even a stick (the United States still had the world's biggest ones) I know not, but insiders say she negotiated brilliantly and Italy got to keep Trieste. (Having argued with her myself, I can attest that she's very good at it; as with Bishop Sheen, there is little in her written work to prepare one for this intellectual rigor.)

Perhaps the last word on Clare's involvement in Italian politics can be left to an Italian wall poster of the period headlined "La Luce Americana Sulla Crisi Italiana." It seems the "American Light" had convoked the ministers of all major parties for a consultation on some government crisis or other and the pantywaists had gone along. No self-respecting Italian should be caught dead discussing internal affairs with a foreign *rappresentante diplomatica*. The poster is the sound of one minor party (maybe Communist—it doesn't say) pouting. Although my Italian stops well short of nuance, there appears nothing sexist about the phrasing: perhaps the reader is expected to supply that himself.

Whether on the strength of the Trieste performance or not, Italy was aligned our way politically when Clare left. The rest, to my parochial mind, is opera. The era of Clare the loner, the battler, is over, and we have instead a crown and a parade, which have been amply covered elsewhere.* Her mother's dreams for her had been nobly fulfilled: a title and a court. Now maybe that side of Clare could rest. (She still seems to enjoy being called Madam Ambassador, but in a way that somehow suggests a fancy-dress party.) The other side, the worker, the old pro, went at it as usual as if it were the only job she'd ever wanted, the thing she was born to do, and undoubtedly ambassadored as well as one can ambassador. This being undoubtedly the case—professionals seemed to respect her, allowing for forked tongues—the only thing left to snipe at her about was her personal behavior which, considering the operators she was dealing with, the fake noblemen and professional charmers that Italy abounds in, seemed remarkably careful and dignified.

Unfortunately, the lead-poisoning episode did much to undo this. I was quite willing to believe that something bad had indeed come down from the embassy ceiling and even that someone might have been out to get her. But I wished it had happened to somebody else. Because her long-dormant record for self-dramatization came rushing back. In the fifties, we were not in the habit of assassinations, and scepticism levels were high. Why, we had never even

* See Alden Hatch, *Ambassador Extraordinary: Clare Booth Luce* for the full brass section. (New York: Holt, Rinehart & Winston, 1956).

heard of lead poisoning in Harlem. As I recall, there were news pictures of a ceiling and a sofa, proving I'm not sure what, and newspaper stories presumably written by men who believed that women, especially Clare, are subject to hot flashes. Public women are well advised to be meticulously prosaic for this reason, a requirement that Clare hasn't always met.

To round out the story, I recently asked her to describe the incident herself. She says that she did try to contain the arsenic report: that she told Eisenhower about it privately with a view to resigning quietly, and that Ike's press secretary Jim Haggerty stuffed it into his next news briefing, and the deed was done. She did not claim that anybody was trying to poison her, only that her behavior was being oddly affected by something—which is borne out by several witnesses who claim that she seemed drunk or on drugs on several social occasions.

Richard Helms of the CIA has since verified that there was indeed arsenic on the ceiling, as there was on many old Italian ceilings, which substance had for centuries given rise to the myth of the deadly Roman night air. The stuff was loosened over Clare's study by the bangings of a laundromat upstairs, and since she was sleeping on the sofa, there was no canopy to intercept it. She says it would take a good hundred years for this level of arsenic to kill you, but it makes you woozy in no time.

Unfortunately, the kind of cleverness Clare practices is a razor's-edge game at best, and a pinch of wooziness throws it completely out of kilter (which is why she *has* to drink moderately: every occasion when she hasn't seems to have been remembered by someone). The scattering of Clare stories out of Rome had her monopolizing people and laying down Luce's Law as never before. The writer Isabella Taves writes to me describing a party someplace on the Tiber: "Madame arrives spaced out . . . it wasn't liquor, but she was being very odd. First, she went on and on about seeing a flying saucer on the Via Veneto, then she began on insulation of airports," at which point the other guests were palpably going nuts, so Miss Taves tried to interject a question. Clare just kept on going, this time about the future of insulated housing, winding up, "Think what this will mean to *us housewives.*"

The next day at the embassy, Miss Taves found Clare as rational as could be, signing off with the telling line, "Tell Fleur [Cowles] it's harder being an Ambassadress than she thinks." It's certainly hard if arsenic is dripping into your brain-pan, and you can't tell anyone about it, because he or she will think it's just another hallucination. Since she and Harry had long since been dubbed "Arsenic and old Luce," the poison on the ceiling provided, so to speak, the icing on the cake.

Weirdly enough, it is both the kind of over-neat story she likes to invent, and the kind people like to believe about her. Arsenic falling on arsenic was just what the legend called for. Her years of silence were forgotten, her good behavior undone. Clare had been carrying on like that for years, everyone knew that. Her image was etched in bronze, and she could only confirm, not alter it, like an ex-con trying to go straight.

She confirmed it in spades in the famous Wayne Morse episode. Again, we'll stick to the view from the bunkhouse. "I see your friend is at it again." Yes indeed. With her Roman stint behind her, Ike had proposed Clare for Ambassador to Brazil in 1959, and Latin America was a funny place to send any kind of Luce. Traditionally, we have treated our subcontinent like a drunken father who ignores the kids himself but who beats the daylights out of anyone else who takes an interest. (See Monroe Doctrine.) And Latin America, sick to death by now of Xavier Cugat and *Flying Down to Rio*, was beginning to resent it. A friend who knows tells me that they still blame everything from the weather to syphilis on the United Fruit Company. And if the Luces weren't quite the UFC, they would do. Besides which, Clare was a beautiful woman, something to be pinched and revered, but surely no more.

So trouble was to be expected, even from the nodding Eisenhower Congress, and Wayne Morse was the natural carrier for it. Morse was one of those people commonly described as uniquely American, because he was so unfathomably peculiar. He was a Far Westerner who comfortably distanced definition. Although one of the two senators to oppose the Tonkin Gulf resolution, Morse could not be contained by the word "liberal." In fact, neither party was big enough for him and he became an independent, which was still putting it mildly. I ran into him years later at the Chicago Democratic Convention of '68, and a more encyclopedic, idiosyncratic political intelligence I never hope to meet.

Clearly not a man to tangle with. If *he* made a mistake, it was just old Wayne up to his tricks; if you made a mistake, you were dead. His opposition to Clare's appointment was, I take it, basically serious. The Luces represented East Coast Republicanism, whose least eloquent spokesman was then Nelson Rockefeller, who was later on in the Eisenhower doldrums pelted with disorganized fruit when he toured Latin America, an indication of what might have happened to Clare (although Nelson invited fruit-throwing to a perhaps unusual degree). But liberal foreign-policy positions had to go in disguise in those days, so Morse dug up those old visits Clare had paid to a psychiatrist in the twenties—just the thing to inflame conservative sentiment in 1957. And Clare responded in kind.

She said in, I take it, her nerve-rackingly sweetest tones that she'd heard that the senator from Oregon had once been kicked in the head by a horse. Pandemonium. Outside of the fact that being kicked by a horse was far more American than seeing a shrink, nobody expected anything else from Morse anyway, it only enriched the legend; but for Clare to wisecrack about it—well, that was Senate confirmation with a vengeance. Bitchy, brittle, everything they'd always suspected. Harry was furious with her, but she says she'd do this one over again with pleasure. In fact, she told intimates that the horse had caught Morse on the right side of the head, and he'd been thinking left ever since: just the soothing words that were needed. At that, the Senate might still have voted her through, but by now the Brazilians were aroused. Morse's task was complete. All he needed was a fuss, any fuss, and Clare had provided it. She withdrew of her own accord, and left the Big Top for good, or so it seemed.

There really was nothing left to prove, except how many things she could do in a lifetime. Although her second tour of the limelight had been much more graceful than her first, she had become such an automatic target that she still couldn't do anything right, as far as her critics were concerned. And her admirers were satisfied with what they had. She was not quitting under fire—if there'd been any hint of that, she'd have stuck around for the hell of it. She was still in her prime, but being famous for the sake of being famous had clearly begun to pall. There were still plenty of famous things to do, but nothing that would add anything. So she decided once more to explore the mysteries of the private life— only a little less exclusively religiously this time. The Church was home now, and there was no need to carry on about it.

On the way to retirement, she discovered scuba diving, a sport like unto a religious conversion or watery rebirth, which its devotees itch to share and relive for you, and Clare peppered a magazine I worked for, called *Jubilee*, with scuba-diving pieces, although we were not strictly an aquatic journal. Characteristically, she also wrote a short story for *Sports Illustrated* about a ghastly older woman who lays down the law about scuba diving so arrogantly and omnisciently that she goads a young man into making a fatal mistake just to defy her. "Yes, that lady was based on me," says Clare the tireless self-parodist.

The underwater vision came just in time, because later she developed cataracts and now has to swim sedately with her head up and straw hat on, like old royalty taking the baths. No more coral kingdoms for her, although one more source of visions lay ahead.

She and Harry got themselves a place in Arizona, a gesture of isolation in itself, although I always pictured Harry summoning Air Force One to whisk him to work. If dull company was a problem for Clare in New York, one imagined a plague-sized epidemic in Phoenix. But my parents who saw them periodically out there reported an unprecedented serenity on Clare's part. She was doing ceramics and painting and a column for *McCall's*: the usual buzz of hobbies. In fact, she worked very hard at her Art, just in case America needed a great painter in a hurry (actually she doesn't have to excel to enjoy doing something). And she was also at some point taking LSD, which can account for a lot of serenity, if it hits you right.

At that time, LSD was almost unknown, so it is nice to think of the Luces blazing a trail for later hippies to follow. The effects on both were benign, and Harry actually strolled out into the backyard (or back ranch) one night conducting an invisible symphony orchestra. Another time he claimed to have talked to God on the golf course, and found that the Old Boy seemed to be on top of things and knew pretty much what He was doing. The old prickly pear had found the right medicine. Clare was equally euphoric, and characteristically tried to pass on the discovery to others, including my mother, a stately but adventurous woman, who would try anything, or at least *think* of trying anything. She finally refrained because of the coincidental heart attacks of two previous converts, the afore-mentioned Fathers Murray and Weigel. A courtly little group of acid droppers if there ever was one, out there in the desert.

"LSD saved our marriage" would be putting it too strongly, but it may have made it a little mellower. Harry had gone through a somewhat restless, tossing-and-turning mid-life, in the course of which in 1959 he had made marrying noises in the direction of one Lady Jean Campbell, the granddaughter of Lord Beaverbrook, the British press baron. Clare knew she herself had few wifely claims on Harry, and has always been very understanding in sexual matters, but she was embarrassed to tears over *Harry*, who appeared to be making an ass of himself, and tangentially herself. (Harry's other wife, Time Inc., felt roughly the same way.)

The best name for her feeling is probably simple confusion. Lady Jean was the least likely suspect, a young girl they'd befriended as a favor to the Beaver, and who had stayed with both of them in the Bahamas a couple of years before, practically a ward of the family, and by the Luces' standards a bit of a toper. Clare had never guessed (and she guessed many things) that anything like this was even possible. Her public response was a superb example of grace under pressure (which is actually the definition of wit, not courage at all). She said, "If Jean marries Henry and I marry Lord Beaverbrook, then I'll be Harry's grandmother."

A playwright's line. *She* stays unruffled, and *he* is caught with his pants down, a foolish old man having a last Highland fling. In reality, though, Clare was plenty ruffled, and she had no desire to humiliate Harry. She told him he could have his divorce if he really wanted it, but first they should confront each other: not for a battle of wills precisely (Harry had all the cards), but a last meeting of minds, of souls. One pictures Harry staring, furrowing, thinking furiously, finally agreeing to forget it.*

The episode sheds some light on Luce. The upstanding fellow who'd allegedly been vamped by Clare, the scheming socialite, in the thirties has to be revised a little. Allowing for the prankish demands of the flesh or a possible flare-up of paternalism (remember how he had loved young Ann), we are left with the fact that Lady Jean had a big-bang title, and that Luce-Beaverbrook would have made a formidable international dynasty. If Clare had made such a match for herself, heads and tongues would have wagged sideways and up and down. Because her once-scandalous romance with Harry was like unto Éloïse and Abélard compared to this number.

However, there's no point throwing stones at Harry. You can't be harder on a good Presbyterian than he is on himself, and after this bizarre lapse, Luce seems to have worked very hard and rewardingly at being a good husband the rest of the way. My parents saw him in Arizona shortly before he died in 1967, and reported a sweetness about him they'd never noticed before. My

---

* In the event, Lady Jean had to settle, like so many others, for a piece of Norman Mailer, who has hinted in his roguish way that he got a kick out of replacing a press lord. Power, baby. On our one meeting, I found Lady Jean a quite unlikely siren: buxom and vivacious but not, visually speaking, the "other woman" of legend. She endeared herself to me forever by saying, "All you Jewish intellectuals are alike"—a compliment I treasure.

mother thought it might be a premonition that he was not long for this world.

So his passing was as painless as such things can ever be: a sudden heart attack visiting a soul at peace, one who had talked in his own odd way to God. It was a consummation and not, as so often in Clare's life, a disaster. But there is no doubt, just from the number and tone of references, that she misses Harry's company very much, his "whut whuts," "very ineressings," and all. A witness tells of seeing Clare weeping openly outside La Grenouille when Harry appeared to have a slight coronary, but looking completely composed when he came out okay. Clare did her crying strictly on her own time.

I ran into Clare in New York sometime during her lotus-land period and I must say she did seem a little spaced out, in a sleepy, cheerful way. To the uninitiated, she might have appeared tipsy, which also is possible, since Clare can be the world's worst lightweight drinker, and a thimbleful of scotch constitutes a skinful. (I know this is often said to cover for real drinkers in politics, but in Clare's case I've seen it myself. I measured the stuff in teaspoons one night and she still got light-headed.) With tales of LSD still fresh in my mind, I suspected a brief return trip, with the drug checking in to see if it had left anything behind.

Whatever it was, it righted itself soon enough. My other contacts with her mostly consisted of phone calls after each of my novels, telling me how good they were, but how *great* the next one was going to be. For an alleged careerist, she is an unflagging booster of others, and really wants all her friends to do as well as she has. Her love of success is not the least piggy. She wants everyone to have a piece. The call I remember best came after a book of mine called *Office Politics*, which was ostensibly about life on a small magazine. "That's just how it was around Harry," she said.

For some reason which may have been completely unconnected with the Luces, I received a summons from *Time* magazine in the early sixties to determine whether I'd like a job there. It was a funny kind of interview, because they kept asking me *why* I wanted a job there, and I kept saying I didn't want one, that *they* had sent for *me*. Well, said they, you'll have to work your tail off, of course, but it'll be well worth it. But, said I, I don't want to work at all, let alone my tail off, whatever the rewards.

The first man, James Shepley, washed his hands of me at that point and sent me up an echelon to, I believe, Roy Alexander, who asked me the same questions. Alexander finally shook his head and sent me yet higher in the castle to Otto Fuerbinger, the Iron Duke, who didn't know why I was there at all. For want of anything better to do, I wound up telling him that his magazine was all wet about Walter Lippmann. He disagreed, mildly enough: *Time* was exactly right about Walter Lippmann, he felt. Also about Joseph Alsop. It was easy enough for me to do, because I really *didn't* want a job there.

Before Luce's successor Henry Grunwald let a hundred flowers bloom later in the decade, Time Inc. had a reputation for castrating writers second to none. There has since been some haphazard revisionism of this—pretty good writers like James Agee, Nigel Dennis, Irving Howe, etc., etc., did survive with their styles intact—but at the time, *Time* was considered the black death by young writers. And as I passed the writers' cubicles, or warrens, that day and saw them all sitting there with their white shirt sleeves tucked halfway up the forearm, I decided these were the exact opposite of my idea of writing conditions, which is to sprawl in maximum disarray. I had also met a *Time* writer once at Ridgefield and he had seemed quite alarmingly mild and sycophantic. (I now know that Luce liked independent chaps who snapped back at him, but this guy was a houseboy.)

Besides, I had vowed not to cash in on the Luce connection in that particular manner. There was no way of deluding oneself that one could remain an equal of whatever sort while serving as an employee. As I say, the Luces may have had nothing to do with my job offer. But the moonstruck quality of my interviews led me to suspect a Luce memo dimly understood. Maybe Harry had barked, "See Sheed. Whut whut," and maybe he hadn't, but I wasn't taking any chances.

Harry died in 1967, taking this minor secret with him, and sometime soon after that I received an invitation from Clare to come see her at the Sherry-Netherland, her New York pad.

After all the talk, I was relieved to find her more or less the way I'd left her, sunny and gentle and life-size. The media monster was nowhere in sight. As pictures will attest, she was as beautiful as ever, although she didn't think so herself. "At my age"—and here I must paraphrase from memory—"the big problem is not accumulating property but getting rid of it. [From experience, I refrained from offering to help.] Fame? I always knew that *that* wouldn't last forever. The night *The Women* opened, I went to the top of the Empire State Building and realized that none of the ants on the street had ever heard of me. So much for being famous. You do miss being recognized at airports and being sent to the head of the line, but that's about all. What I do miss is my looks."

Since literally this was preposterous, I had to assume she meant the galvanic quality—"sex appeal" is too neutral a term— that had sent her into orbit in the first place. Heads used to swivel regardless of gender when Clare entered a room. Fame is, as Herr Kissinger tells us, the greatest aphrodisiac, so the two losses may have been somewhat connected. Yet Clare had formerly affected to resent being famous for her looks (see "legs v. other end") and she couldn't have it both ways, could she? "It's very hard for a hand-some man to be taken seriously," my father once told me (in refer-ence to Robert Hutchins of Chicago U.), and this surely goes triple for handsome women. So Clare might have felt well rid of her in-candescence, to see how she'd do without it. Perhaps she could move into a think tank now, or become like Baruch, an advisor to Presidents—antic thoughts that were not so far off the mark as I supposed.

What I didn't know then was that Clare had written an article for *Life* not too long before about the death of Marilyn Monroe, in which she ascribed its cause precisely to the loss of beauty. At some one moment, she says, looking in the mirror ceases to be a comfort for a woman and becomes "a summit conference with the enemy." Hollywood did not kill Marilyn, according to Clare; if anything, it kept her alive by confirming so opulently what she saw in the glass and refracting it coast to coast. But when that went, she went.

The essay undoubtedly has the extra spin on it of personal identification. At least while writing it, Clare seems to have felt her way into the situation almost as fully as Norman Mailer. Luce's Marilyn, a fellow waif, could barely get enough assurance from a howling mob, let alone one man. Pluckily she tried other interests, but they all came back to the mirror. When the last wolf whistle had died, what use were other interests? I think what Clare was telling me that day was that while she herself obviously had inter-ests galore, it was still tough to lose the looking-glass war. She wasn't that much better than old Marilyn.*

Clare may have had a tough five minutes or more with the problem, maybe as far back as the time I knew her, maybe further.

---

* Recently she told me that Marilyn's embalmer had found her toenails uncared for, a sure sign of neurosis: especially since the studio took responsibility for all the rest of her. *That* is the kind of other interest that, perhaps, distinguishes Clare from Miss Monroe.

It is more a premonition than a reality, like seeing a skeleton in the looking glass, and in the article she says it can hit you anytime after thirty, which gives us a lot of years to play with.

It certainly didn't seem to weigh too heavy today: obviously she still went to the front of the line everywhere, and heads still turned, if more slowly. It was more a resumption of our old pas-time—spitballing rumination about life in general. At some point, we were interrupted by a phone call, which Clare answered like the first scene of a musical. " 'Allo, 'allo? She ees no 'ere. Ah tell 'er you call." Fifi the French maid returned to her seat and resumed our conversation.

We talked about war, and she defended Vietnam in passing on the grounds of mysterious global policy needs which she was not about to pass on. She seemed to have become terrifically knowing and inscrutable about Asian affairs, which seems literally to go with the territory. Although she claimed that the famous China lobby was just a bunch of regular guys, it was by the nature of the case also packed with yesteryear's China experts, and an expert never knows when to quit. Since I couldn't very well argue with a myste-rious policy need, I let it pass. Now, as for the killing over there, she asked—was it really worse than letting people die in a hospital strike? Well yes, I thought later, inflicting death is still worse than not preventing it. But at the time, I mumbled something about how it takes two to make a strike, and she agreed affably, since I had just played straight into her court.

The subject of killing got us back into her stream of rumina-tion. She said that her experience as a war correspondent in China in 1942 had been so horrifying that she had had to harden herself like a professional nurse. She supposed that particular part of her-self had remained hard. But she remembered the horror, too, of pain and rotting flesh, and I gathered she was not one of your bloodthirsty hawks. I know this will seem ingenuous to people who've been banged about by her rhetoric, but in private I've never sensed a taste for battle, only for its foreplay. Although as we shall see, she loves the military, it is for its latent power, its violence under wraps. I can just see Clare in the War Room pushing count-ers triumphantly over the map, proving the superiority of her "other end" in one more sphere. But it would be more like jigsaw puzzling than war. In real life her main war-related activity for the past few years has been East Asian refugee relief—maybe in mem-ory of China, 1942.

Unfortunately, I didn't know I was going to write a book about her, so the rest of the lunch tends to dissolve on me. We had some wine, which we never had with Harry, but otherwise the clock was turned back, and I could have been sitting on the patio in Ridgefield chewing the fat as we did in the Summer of 1949. She wanted to know if life had surprised me in any way, and how the days passed for a penny-a-line scribbler. And we talked about the odds on second marriages working (only so-so, given mankind's repetitiousness). She did not talk about herself at all, after that opening burst, and she might as well never have been to Rome, or almost to Brazil.

A few days later, she asked me to be her partner at a dinner at William F. Buckley's. Buckley, as rumored, is a crypto-nice guy (there's nothing libelous about that, is there?). As a Tory Christian, he has no choice. It is his duty. If you believe that neither government nor business should help people, you put an awful strain on private virtue. But anyone who says things like "noblesse oblige" as often as Bill is obviously equal to it. First among his graces, as far as I'm concerned, is that from the start he has abstained from mentioning politics to me, except in the grossest spirit of raillery and frat-house kidding. Indeed, he sometimes makes politics seem like a nine-to-five chore that he is happy to shrug out of at day's end. Perhaps for this reason, his more right-wing pieces tend to remind me of someone talking extra-loud to a rich relative who must be kept in a good humor. "Big Government. I said, '*Big Government*'!"

Be that as it may, tonight belonged to Clare anyway. She held forth about the state of the world in a manner so unlike her lunchtime self that my mind was wrenched back to the other Clare, the autocrat at the dinner table. I believe she was doing her number about how people think wealth is a pyramid, whereas it is really more like an egg. Later I asked Buckley what he made of Clare and he said, "One just sits back in wonder."

Overwhelming Buckley is not as hard as it seems, if there are no microphones handy. At his own place, he almost invites other people to shine. But Clare didn't need an invitation. She would have shone at a pit auction. Her style was the rather old-fashioned one of setting up a topic and inviting everyone to speak to it. I remember on a later occasion her asking the table if anyone recalled precisely the exact moment he or she learned how to read: that kind of topic. It put me in mind of the inveterate games her show-business friends used to play after dinner—no evening was complete without them—and I realized that this was the nearest equivalent in a stuffy world. Harry had introduced her to staider company, but she still wanted her fun. And concocting theories was the closest thing to charades.

This cast a pleasant light back on those curious dinners at Ridgefield. Clare was a theater person dragged into an old men's club, but she refused to let it cramp her style. Global thinking could be a game, forecasting universal doom could be a glorious game. The fact that nobody else was playing might make her look like a show-off; but she *wanted* them to play. She listened closely and laughed quickly at the least hint of someone else's cleverness. In the parched air of big shots, she treasured wit wherever she found it.

Hence Buckley. This mellow evening gave me a chance to catch up with the company Clare was keeping and the positions her public myth was taking. Legend to the contrary, I had never thought of her as precisely a label-bearing conservative before she started writing for Buckley's *National Review* in the sixties. The very term endangered her unexpectedness. But she wanted friendships and alliances—she hates being ineffectual—and here she had the most congenial. Buckley, the old CIA hand, always seems to be at the center of things. If you want to meet the liberal establishment, go to his place. There a J. K. Galbraith and a Milton Friedman may be heard discussing ski slopes or whatever, while outside the Archie Bunkers or foot soldiers of bigotry slug it out over doctrine. The top people have no need to shout; they leave that to the servants.

This is a great scandal to the average citizen: Jack Kennedy *couldn't* have liked Joe McCarthy; Clare Luce couldn't have liked Harry Bridges. No disclosures, I have found, cause greater shock or disbelief than these odd-shoe friendships. Yet they are essential to understanding Clare's world.

As I remembered, and was to learn again in Honolulu, not all of Clare's circles carry this Athenian atmosphere. On the Rich Man's Right, even a wishy-washy liberal (but I repeat myself, as Mark Twain might say) feels like an enemy spy. The truisms of the profit system are as unquestioned over there as the truisms of public welfare used to be at West Side cocktail parties in New York. It occurs to me that if Clare has to spend much time with that gang, Buckley's place must seem like a veritable redoubt of free inquiry.

Because, as later visits with Bill have confirmed, it is here that one occasionally meets the mythical center, the place where the people who run things can assemble and discuss current events with as much or little ideology as they unspokenly decide. It is amazing how many public matters, from détente to busing, can be nonideologically discussed if they have to be, i.e., by people who have to do something about them. On the businessman's right, contrariwise, one sometimes senses the gloom of people who have heard a deathwatch beetle in the attic. It may take centuries to reach the living room, but the rot is on its way. So, in the most tooth-watering surroundings, they sit braced for defeat—at the hands of the state, the unions, even the gold-digging unemployed. This would be bad company for Clare, retired fighter and power person. I don't really know whether the bouncy *National Review* is any closer to Power than these aging mourners, but it retains, at least in its chief, the theatrics of power, and it charges Clare's batteries agreeably.

Anyway, it was not a particularly political evening, unless the great egg-pyramid question is so construed, or a quaint exchange I had with my breathtaking hostess, Pat Buckley (She: "So-and-so worked like a nigger for Nixon." Me: "That wouldn't get you very far with Nixon." She: "I won't even dignify that with a titter." I print this only because Pat is not only preternaturally kind in real life but quite without hypocrisy, and would print it herself, if she thought it worth dignifying) and I still didn't think of Clare as preeminently political at that point. She likes conversation wherever it takes her, as if it were an organized idea-hunt with everybody beating the bushes lustily. It is not, I decide, regretfully, a lazy man's game.

I don't really care where Clare is going politically, perhaps because that side of her has never struck me as particularly important (which may tell something about her different modes of friendship). If she has missed connections with the Catholic Left, Buckley's part-Catholic Right will do. I am happy to see that jaunty flag still flying, wherever it chooses. Regarding which, I get a most eccentric reassurance about Clare, that perhaps reassures only me, a year or so later when I chance upon an answer she has given to one of her myriad interviewers. The question might be considered a trick one, being addressed to a pillar of the Church and all that, to wit: "Do you think sex is dirty?" Imagined pause as Clare decides how to dispose of the popinjay.

"I don't know if it's dirty," she drawls. "But it certainly is smelly." It took me right back.

# CHAPTER SEVEN

# *Winter 1977*

The legend ossifies. The critics have all gone home or are doing something else. The aforementioned Stephen Shadegg writes a pious little book about her in 1970 that reads like a press release and I lash out at it peevishly in *The New York Times,* and then when one W. A. Swanberg writes a laborious biography against Harry Luce, I take a swing at that, too, although God knows Luce meant little enough to me by that time. Still, one wants to set these things straight.

Then good old Helen Lawrenson did a rehash in *Esquire* of all the nasty things people used to say about Clare, and it sounded as if it might be the last word. It seemed silly for me to weigh in yet again like some doddering caretaker. Lawrenson knew Clare at a time when Clare herself had admitted to being pretty awful. So who knows? I spotted one story in Lawrenson that belongs by rights to somebody else: about how Clare would invite one famous person over on the pretext that another famous person was coming, until she had her whole party. This had always struck me as a pretty spunky thing to do, but as I say, it's a chestnut. By the time in question, the rich, beautiful Clare could hardly have needed such ruses to fill a room, though she might have done them for fun. You wouldn't guess it from Lawrenson, but Clare is an intermittent leg-puller and not *always* the victim of jokes.

More mysterious yet, Lawrenson described trekking up to Ridgefield year after year with her labor leader husband Jack, even though she was bored, had nothing in common with Clare, lived by different values, and was an altogether finer person. Unless she went up there to sneer at Clare's values, it's hard to understand why she bothered to make the trip at all. Most such pilgrims tended to be looking for handouts, or gathering notes for a hatchet job (which may be why the Rich are so trusting), but presumably neither of these would apply to Lawrenson or her husband, good old no-nonsense Jack.

The settling of old scores generally leaves out something important, and we'll just have to guess why Clare attracts the kind of enemy that keeps in touch so faithfully before beating her up so thoroughly. The book version of Lawrenson seemed milder than the *Esquire* one, either because it was slightly softened or because I was getting used to it. The only thing that still bothered me was Lawrenson's gift, almost akin to Lillian Hellman's, for making herself seem like *your kind of guy* in some gritty, down-to-earth way. So anyone she dislikes must be flashy, phony, definitely nongritty.

If this *was* going to be the last word about Clare—and since Lawrenson writes rings around most anybody, it might well be—it would leave a nasty stain. All that crazy striving and struggling and nothing but this to show for it.

As a ritual murder, Lawrenson's memoir intrigued me the more I thought about it. As a young career girl herself, Helen Norden Brown had gotten her job at *Vanity Fair* from Clare and was helped by her in other ways. In fact, Clare even served as godmother to Lawrenson's daughter, which makes Clare, as she might say, Abbie Hoffman's godmother-in-law. But at some point Lawrenson chose the acceptable female role of sniping (which is why Dorothy Parker wins her anecdotes with Clare, too) instead of competing, and of immersing herself in her husband's life, while Clare went careening along as herself. It must have been tempting indeed for Lawrenson to shoot her old patroness on the wing.

Politically, Lawrenson functions off and on as a sort of Social Register of the Left. Her role as such is to see through middle-class disguises and report them immediately to the real people—who, by the way, are all splendid (*the only guys I liked there were the ones in the mailroom* kind of thing, done comically often). As a rebel of unimpeachable Wasp stock, Lawrenson is always on the prowl for *arri-*

*vistes.* She once even reproved Fred Astaire for hanging out with the
Whitneys, as if Fred could have developed that style just as well in
Hell's Kitchen. And Clare, while Waspy enough for two, had certainly gone up in the world. So it was almost Lawrenson's duty to
reveal the scurvy details to the rest of us.

In the flesh, Lawrenson also succeeded Clare at the feet of Bernard Baruch (though she probably preferred his gardener and his
valet—one simply marvels at her masochism in hanging around the
rich) and had worked with Clare at a time when *The Women* was
gestating, so that her piece might almost be called "The Revenge of
the Women." Very effective, in any event, and all the old nastiness
about Clare came back for a day in full flower like the village of
Brigadoon.

Time, then, to go take another look for myself.

Clare had long since moved to Hawaii, to a place Harry had
chosen in his later reflective period. Since the time now was the
winter of 1977 and the snow had sealed up my back door tight, my
trip was easier to explain than Ms. Lawrenson's. "Do you want first
or second class?" asked the durable Dorothy Farmer.

"Second," I said, figuring that I'd keep a pinch more integrity
in second. Clare must be used to having to fly out the occasional
pauper if she wants company, and the whole process is very graceful. On the way back, we would simply be handed first-class tickets
and no questions asked.

It's late as my wife and I land in Oahu and are greeted by
Clare's chauffeur, who drapes leis on us—something everybody in
Hawaii from mighty to humble seems equipped to do at a moment's notice—and hands us a card, which says, Aloha, sorry I can't
make it to the airport, but you'll have more room in the car without
me, love, Clare, or words to that effect. *Aloha?* Anyhow, the car is a
Chevy Caprice with 16,000 miles on it, a far cry from the limousines Harry used to hide in the corners of. There are no other cars
in the garage, and the chauffeur is only a part-time employee. So
there is no conspicuous consumption and perhaps, it occurs to me,
not all that much wealth either: not super, gaseous wealth.

It's hard to judge her house at night, except to say that it's sufficiently oriental, like the house in Ridgefield, and that there are a
couple of verbose tropical birds in the atrium that can frighten the
whiskers off the unwary. Tomorrow or sometime I'll take a closer
look.

Clare greets us herself with another "Aloha," which must be
habit-forming, her appearance miraculously unchanged except for

the depth of her glasses and a sense of greater whiteness about her face and hair. Those nine cataract operations have left her partially blind, but she uses what's left with great dexterity, bluffing her way merrily through movies and other spectacles. ("I try to remember to face the screen.") Right now she takes us back to the kitchen, where we forage in the icebox and she apostrophizes the various items: macadamia nuts, macadamia nut cakes, odd bits of cheese. Clare has obviously taken to kitchens since I knew her, which automatically means an interest in the small idiosyncrasies of these places. Despite her failing sight, Clare seems to have a story to tell about every inch of the icebox.

We repair to her lanai (why does Hawaiian always sound like something made up in the Disney Studios?) and discuss the ethnic constitution of the islands, the case for first strike capability and our sleeping arrangements. There is again no break at all between this conversation and our last one. My wife is swept into it like an old friend, and we each seem to get exactly one third of the talking time, although I pass for now on first strike capability. Afterwards Clare tells me, like a good hostess, that my wife seems just right for me. Hah!

Clare shows us our room, with the usual asides about its foibles. There is an intercom, and a somewhat jocose list of all the things you can shout into it, including demands for sleeping pills and breakfast in bed. Since the staff is both small and asleep, I imagine chaos if one acted on this: but it's nice to conjure a world where such things are even contemplated. The next day she points out gleefully that if *her* connection were ever left open, she could hear every word we said. So I test this that very night the only possible way, by saying some terrible things about her. If she heard them, she must be a very good sport.

We are also given a choice between air-conditioning and the thermostatically controlled weather of Hawaii. But we must decide now, because once the windows are shut that's it for the night. All kinds of electronic rigging goes into effect, and if it is nudged, the yard will immediately be aswarm in cops in flowered shirts (or so I imagine). The house fronts onto the sea, and any old beachcomber might be tempted to have a look inside. In fact, Clare claims two minor breakins before the system was installed, though nothing was missing.

This seems fair enough at first, and only by next evening does one realize how cramping such precautions can be. Because it isn't just the windows. By nine o'clock or so, whole areas of the house are sealed off by shatter-proof glass, including the living room, and you have to rustle up a sleepy servant if you want to use the swimming pool. This may sound like a rather precious complaint. But the tyranny of security is felt in its minor annoyances, like bureaucracy. Clare obviously has to live like this, there is no manifest paranoia about it, and she is quite as free as she wants to be. But living like a crown jewel must surely affect one's political philosophy slightly every time one turns the switch that seals one off from the world.

Or so it seems if you're new to it. Clare has been rich and beautiful for a long time, and must take being Queen of the Jungle in her stride by now. The real wall between her and the rest of us is not an electric screen but wealth and beauty themselves and the life these inexorably fashion for one; so if you're not rich or beautiful, not at all like a crown jewel, you feel silly being locked up at night.

The days fall into a perfect-day pattern right away, as they did at Ridgefield: as though having found a good way to spend the day, or feed Harry, or whatever, one saw no need to change it. In the morning one works, in the afternoon one swims—sedately now, because she mustn't get her eyes wet, and with a mock dignity— and in the evening one talks. Clare is exceedingly orderly, and the only thing that breaks the shape of time is an "event"—a speech, a reception—to which blessedly she is also addicted. Otherwise, she finds no monotony in repetition. Her mother, remember, was German-American, and in this respect so is Clare. Her punctuality is frightening, geared to seconds, not minutes, and though she blames it on Harry, who won her heart by whipping out his watch at their first two meetings and snapping, "It's past my bedtime," she must have been quite a study. Maybe being a punctual woman was considered another first by the wags of her day. Or maybe she remembers being late for her first Washington press conference and paying for it in bad notices. But Clare can be as shifty about all this as a secret drinker. "My cook gets noivous," she says as she marches you toward the dining room, although her cook seems a monument of placidity.

Anyway, lunch is always at twelve sharp, whether she has it with us or not, and supper is on the dot of seven. Her own lunch and my wife's are designed for a dieter's pecking, but my own plate is full to bursting, and I alone am brought wine, in a small fish-shaped carafe. "It's good to have a man in the place again," she says, and I realize with a bump that this trail-blazing feminist still has a nearly oriental style with men. I can well believe the hitherto unlikely story that Harry liked to walk a few feet in front of her in public; and I can see how this geisha approach could have maddened whole generations of women.

Yet Clare has always had close women friends who get displaced only when the great tidal wave of a man enters, and not always then. She is just as happy with girl talk as she is discussing portfolios with fat cats. Only occasionally is one reminded of the inevitable barriers. "We must be on time for dinner tonight at so-and-so's, because the poor girl has to do her own cooking." (My wife trembles visibly.) Or speaking of portfolios, she told me that the surest way to break the ice at a party is to ask someone about *his*—as if everyone in God's green world had a portfolio.

There is not much middle class in Clare's world, or, as far as I can make out, on Oahu itself, which is a military base set in a nest of millionaires. And if Clare can't help sounding rich after fifty years of it (I never knew anyone who could), it is partly because she probably has no idea whether the rest of us have money or not. As in the English gentry, one talks as if everyone had a bit. We agree that taxes are wiping us all out, though Clare pays her accountant maybe $10,000 a year to retard this, and I pay mine somewhat less. She knows enough about the price of hamburger to marvel at how the average housewife gets by at all: although she eulogizes coming up the hard way, she clearly wouldn't care to try it again. She also believes that her kind of money will definitely not last another generation, and she has the imagination and memory to know what this means. "For the first time in my life, most of the people I know do not want to see the future," she said. "Do you?" I reminded her that I had children, and she said that that gave me seventy-five years of future to care about. After the grandchildren, I wouldn't give a damn either.

Although the rich have been known to tremble even in nine figures, Clare's flippant gloom is not unrealistic. She is indeed not super-rich, I gather, and can see the ground, still some distance, underneath. She expressed mild annoyance over Harry for leaving whatever he left her in trusts—because it was such a typical male thing to do. Perhaps Harry was still reeling from that mythical day in Tiffany's ("Are we rich or aren't we?"), but Clare is no spendthrift now.

I reflect that I am now precisely the age Clare was when I met her that Summer. It's chastening to think that, back then, I was barely aware of money. The change is in me.

Anyway, to wrap that up: while Clare seems to act richer at

some times than at others, at no time does she fail to seem something else as well, a fellow-writer or outside observer or whatever it
is we are. That remains her lodge, and even at the stuffiest portfolio
klatsch she can stick her head out and remind you of it with some
wisecrack. At the couple of businessmen's dinner parties we went
to, she gave me the impression we were watching them together
from a phantom press box, and later she talked about the guests as
satirically as a writer should. Although she had led many lives, she
hasn't shed them: she just puts one on top of another.

Sometime after supper on most nights, she hops into bed,
where she perches in a pastel tableau of royalty and I trundle in the
tape recorder and we go at it electronically. As soon as the tape
starts rolling, her voice changes slightly to the public one, and so do
her thoughts. Playing one of the tapes back, she says, "I sound like
a sex-starved spinster. Which perhaps I am." But she says this *in her
normal voice*, which is perhaps uncapturable on tape. It is a soft voice
with one slight impediment—a tendency to slur the *r*'s, making, for
example, "drink" into something like "dink"—which gives it a kittenish flirtatious quality. Clare says Harry used to laugh at it.

"Goodness, that does sound dramatic," she says at another
point. And that tends to be true of all the fourteen or so hours of
tape we did. At the click of the button, she would begin to marshal
her thoughts, almost as though she were reading them—a phenomenon that clearly fascinated her, too. She would also begin slightly
to censor them for the airwaves. In the shadow of Watergate, perhaps anything on tape seemed halfway into the law courts. And
when she came to anything controversial, she automatically turned
off the mike. "Does that mean I can't use this?" "No, no," she said,
and left it at that. Presumably I could use it, but the attribution
would be slightly blurred.

So my notebook, for all its illegibility, brings back Clare more
vividly than her own words when I play them over now. The Clare
of the notebook is the more human and unexpected: if you change
your voice enough, perhaps you do become another person. Clare's
public self may be primarily a vocal condition, from which all else
follows.

At the couple of dinners she gave, the Clare of the tapes tended
to take over again. (I noted in her edition of Emily Post's Etiquette
that the section on dinner parties is heavily underlined, so perhaps
she used the book for more than just research for *Stuffed Shirts*. The
dinners are at any rate wearyingly correct, for a man who still owns
that 1949 dinner jacket.) The taped Clare wants to talk about

first strike capability and the Committee for the Current Danger. The notebook Clare talks about her mother and her brother and the oddities of Harry Luce. Her remark, cited earlier, that "if you married Harry, you became a Republican," saved me hours of deep analysis with the Lady of the tapes, who would have given me 101 profound reasons for becoming a Republican.

And just as she would turn off the set to become intimate, she would turn it on again to become remote. Not that she feared intimacy, far from it, but she had a burning desire to record her global notions one more time. Oddly enough she still considers politics a second-rate vocation. But as a hobby, it is irresistible. It keeps her in action, and she wants to be written about in action. She does not want a book of sage old reflections. And she does not want a "woman's book." She wants her very latest ideas to be in the foreground.

This is ironic. The private life seems to me epic and unique, while a unique idea is almost impossible to come by in a crowded world. And why *these* ideas? She certainly feels a duty to warn the Republic, but also a recurrent hopelessness about this that negates the effort. Ah, what Spengler hath wrought. His shadow falls across the sunniest day. Clare says that the Western civilization which we know will not endure for long, whatever happens: it has run through its life cycle and all the talk in the world won't change that. And although its replacement may be very interesting in its way, there's not much she can do about that either. Her role is to shore up the old order a little longer, not to influence the new one, because she will have nothing in common with it, and therefore nothing to say to it. She decidedly will not play Polonius to a generation of strangers. On the same principle, she likes old friends, because there is no other kind. That at least would be the mood one evening; I call it now her Hawaiian mood, because I haven't heard quite this note of all-the-canoes-are-sinking on the mainland.

Strangely enough, even in this deep-purple phase, Clare does not sound particularly worried about the end of the world: it is rather as though she has solved a particularly vexing puzzle and is pleased and relieved to see where the last piece goes. The occasional exuberance of her gloom reminded me once more of Whittaker Chambers sonorously rediscovering the Decline of the West and playing it on his mighty Wurlitzer. Segments of the Right Wing to which Clare adheres thrive on despair: Kissinger is positively jolly about it. And any account of Clare in her high-security Shangri-la must take note of her vitality.

It's not precisely that despair keeps her young (she would always find a way to do that) but belonging to a brotherhood of despair has its merry moments. The night that Edward Teller dropped in was a good illustration. The Father of the H-bomb was washing his hands terminally over our energy policy, and one couldn't ask for a cheerier evening. Teller was on the island to look into windmill power—now, *that* would be something to be the Father of— and the excitement of this quest shone through the standard pessimism. I sensed, as so often, a gut feeling on the despairing Right that American ingenuity will outwit the politicians at least a few more times. And exaggerating the odds against this adds to the gaiety.

The same phenomenon took a different form one afternoon when a couple of cranks came round to display, in a very top-secret, can-we-trust-your-friend? manner, a solid gold, battery-operated car engine that would, they said, stop the oil crisis cold. Never mind that it required a space like unto a camel's hump to contain it, and that its ultimate cost would at least match the highest gas prices—it was a breakthrough, any breakthrough.

What interested me was that, despite her polite enthusiasm, I never doubted Clare thought they were cranks too. But she was delighted that this kind of American still existed, and that any one of them might come up with the necessary miracle.

And not just in technology. We also looked in on her neighbor William Simon, our bouncy ex-Secretary of Commerce (who has kept bouncing), and found the same mixture of what Paul Valéry called glandular optimism and intellectual pessimism. Simon is the kind of fellow who talks about "political hard ball," and he'd recently played this game in Washington and lost badly, and was now returning to the real world of business, which was also in a bad way. But he exuded an eagerness beyond anything that you're likely to find on the utopian Left.

So pitching in with her quota of cataclysmic prediction could be Clare's way of paying dues to the despair club, as well as a grand new after-dinner game. I have long since given up trying to tell from the noise at dinner parties who's winning the Survival of the West and who's losing. With Clare, if the conversation is good enough, she can face any disaster. And judging from the grunts of approval, this plays very well in Honolulu. When she describes to Edward Teller her theory of first strike capability the wily scientist says, "I don't necessarily agree with you, but I think *somebody* should say those things." In other words, you go first, Clare. (Teller also says that the Inquisition was probably right to suppress Galileo: which may help to explain his own position in the Oppenheimer case.)*

But Clare's obsession with first strike capability goes back a lot deeper than chic pessimism, and plunges us willy-nilly back into the Private. The theory, simply stated, is that democracies are always at a crippling disadvantage, because they can never strike first. Owing to our Christian fussiness about Just Wars, we are obliged perennially to concede the first punch; and the enemy gets to choose the time and place for it. Which means that we must always be more armed-to-the-teeth than the other fellow. Yet this is precisely what democracies are disinclined to bother with.

Thus, if we don't strike while we're ahead, we are absolutely bound to lose to the Kremlin eventually. I suggested that, in a pinch, we could always arrange to have a ship sunk, which usually zips us into war in no time, but she felt that this quaint method would take too long these days. First Strikes have been refined considerably since Pearl Harbor, and you shouldn't go courting one. (Of course, you can always start fighting and *then* have a ship sunk, as in Vietnam.)

But my story here is not our personal pirouettes around geopolitics. Clare's foreign policy is perfectly, even wearyingly, rational: I myself don't care for arguments that can't be settled in three moves (it usually means that someone has misplayed), but clearly this one can't, and so one's mind wanders behind the scenery to find where the ideas come from, in their aesthetic aspect. What experience of life and what fruits of introspection have led Clare so certainly into her implacable-enemy theory: i.e., that one's enemy not only never rests or changes heart, but is bound to win, because in the end Decency won't fight back?

The conviction that the other fellow will hit you if you don't hit him first is the very core of *The Women*, which she wrote long before she began to major in politics. In that play, the heroine does

---

* The Galileo case is, I gather, generally misunderstood. So one can't be dead sure what Dr. Teller thought he was saying. As I understand it, Galileo had been instructed that he must not teach Copernican physics but that he could use them as a hypothesis. The Aristotelian establishment felt that even this was too much and they hollered for the Inquisition to referee in its rough way. The latter, with three negative votes out of ten, judged against Galileo. Teller's testimony in the famous security hearings of his colleague Oppenheimer would have been exactly what the Inquisition ordered: vague feelings of disturbance, puzzlement, nothing concrete. But perhaps you don't get to be the Father of Anything if you don't know that much diplomacy.

what a democracy should, fighting evil with evil, while somehow remaining good. Clare learned all about the preemptive first strike in Newport and Park Avenue, and politics for most of us is partly a projection of private experience (against what other reality could one test it?). When Munich and the fall of France came along, at a most formative moment, they must have seemed like perfect examples writ large of what happens to a person who gives up too easily: a woman, say, who surrenders her husband or is intimidated by Vanderbilts. It is a perfectly valid intuition, and not the least hysterical. ("We did not consider her a silly woman," says a Democrat who served with her recently on a presidential advisory committee). The experience of the thirties, when there *was* an implacable beast at large, made Clares of us all (even small fry) for a time. The difference is one of intensity. Hitler now seems like a bad dream to most people. To Clare, he's a constant possibility. She believes in the Devil.*

Her famous articles in *McCall's* magazine on why she became a Catholic can also be read as a roundabout prologue to her later politics: the problem of evil, in the world and in ourselves, cannot be negotiated, it has to be fought. You can't do business with Hitler, any more than you can do business with the Women. It has nothing to do with hatred: human nature, given certain temptations, will do certain things. Russia will take Europe, as naturally as a man takes a woman. "Up to the age of forty or so, I was surprised when a man *didn't* make a pass at me," she says.

This is not everyone's experience, of course, any more than having people sniff around your money is everybody's experience. And individuals can have both experiences without necessarily wanting to beef up our military budget. But Clare is a *fighter*, if only from memory, and defense spending is a fine manly thing to fight about (why do I picture a nineteenth-century print of a bare-knuckle boxer taking his stance?). Although she quit the ring a long time ago, Clare is like an old champ who still hangs around the gym reminding kids to keep their guard up. Also like a champ, she is incurably genial, having long since worked out her aggressions, if one can use such a flat phrase for such boisterous goings-on. It is

---

* Back in the forties, Spyros Skouras commissioned Clare to help make a movie out of C. S. Lewis' *Screwtape Letters*, which is an imaginary correspondence between the Devil and his nephew Screwtape. It soon became clear that Skouras wanted a devil on the lines of a Halloween prankster, so Clare had to keep saying, but the Devil wouldn't *do* that, until they must have thought she was possessed herself. (That the Devil doesn't have nephews either is another story.) Fortunately the movie came to nothing.

the game itself that she loves. She admits she has become much more at peace with the world and herself, and her saber-rattling seems almost playful, to the point of seeming unfelt. "I'm happier than I ever was, because I don't have nightmares anymore," she says surprisingly, but leaves it at that.

Clare has always sounded flippant because we all tend to go with the style that worked first, and hers was laced with the smart chat of *Vanity Fair* and the twenties in general. But if this style once stood sentry over real hardness and bitterness, these have long since dissolved: Clare is a good winner, and there are no prisoners tied to her chariot. "I don't have any warm personal enemies left," she laments. "All the SOB's have died."

But in fact, she seems to have made peace anyway with most of her SOB's, dead or alive. She tells gleefully of hatchet-buryings with the likes of Hubert Humphrey and Henry Wallace, complete with whatever apologies were felt in order. Helen Lawrenson? "A nice, smart girl. I always liked her." Peacemaking is her latest hobby, and she is as thorough as ever about it. Unlike Mr. Nixon, she really seems beyond resentment: or if there *is* any left over, she can always take it out on the Soviet Union.

If this sounds a little sanctimonious, a little too much Hawaiian poi poi, I should add that she's still as funny as ever about people's mannerisms, etc., including dear Harry's, and that she can get genuinely sore when *friends* are treated badly (she gloated the old way when a pol who'd seduced a friend of hers to advance himself was indicted and found to be homosexual to boot). But she firmly lays off the hard stuff, the uncut malice. Over many hours and several drinks, she never once cracked or blurted an unkindness, although she did admit, under grueling interrogation, that she thought Otto Preminger had gone further on less talent than anyone she had ever met. That was her limit. And when her old sparring partner William Fulbright heaved up on the lanai one day and they embraced like high school sweethearts, prior to tête-à-têting for hours, I realized there was no point looking for any more arsenic around here. She might still think Fulbright a political jackass (I honestly don't know) but any enemies list has long since been burned and forgotten.

The enemy now is mankind's last one, boredom, and it's a hard fight when you're half-blind and living on Hawaii—the Dantesque resort of people who follow the sun, only to find each other. But she manages.

She does not do it by living in the past. As I say, we have to

wade through an awful lot of defense spending to get to that particular door. But when we do, she does not flinch from it. The past is
an old friend and an enemy, and a lover, an entertaining lot as she
describes them.

With godchild Clare Boothe Carey

Portrait of the artist as a
young freeloader, 1949

Clare in *Candida*, 1945

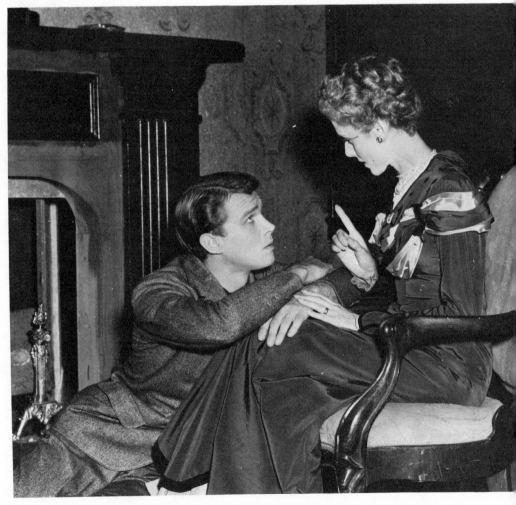

An unusual picture of my father, Frank Sheed. "A fat man owes it to society never to take his coat off."

Earthly powers:
Nelson Rockefeller,
Francis J. Spellman, LBJ

"But your holiness, I too am a Catholic," Clare and Pius XII

Clare and Winston Churchill, 1954

The Ambassador at Assisi, the shrine of Saint Clare

Eisenhower, Luce, Dulles at requiem for Pius XII (1958)

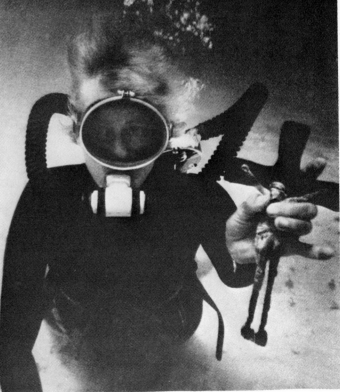

Clare and the Sea

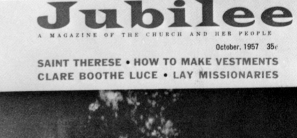

Cover feature: Clare Boothe Luce's "Diary of a Diver"

*Jubilee Magazine, 1957*

Alfred Eisens

Lord Beaverbrook who, with a little help, could have made Clare Harry's grandmother; see p. 125

Clare with her favorite army, Mark Clark's Fifth

Clare's paintings lose a little in black and white

Clare and Eleanor, two kinds of distinction

The private face in the public place: Clare on William Buckley's television show

Receiving Sylvanius Thayer award at West Point, 1979

(*overleaf*) Clare and the bird in Hawaii, 1977

# CHAPTER EIGHT

# *Winter and After: The Battle of Boredom*

"A fur-lined rut" is how Clare describes her life in Hawaii. So why does she do it?

Well, to begin with, she doesn't live there completely. She comes to the mainland every few months for an "intellectual fix": politics in Washington (what else?) and "other things" in New York. This last sounds a bit defiant, because to my ear she talks politics in New York too, partly because people talk them to her. Politics is such an easy peg, a thinking man's weather, and so many other pegs are gone: in Hollywood, Rosalind Russell, Irene Dunne, Loretta Young (the Catholic Mafia); for Broadway, the roll call would be longer and more painful. But politicians either last forever or are replaced by duplicates, so that's where the old friends are in greatest bulk.

Hawaii is to some extent a charming counsel of despair, and Clare talks periodically of making her getaway. Until recently, she kept an apartment in the rascally old Watergate, but for practical reasons too dull to go into, she gave it up. Besides, Washington really rubs your nose in politics and won't quit, like the fat disconsolate bully it is. New York is both more seductive and more difficult to cope with, for reasons that have been sufficiently aired in film and story. One forces oneself now and then to remember that

this woman looking at me so intently is half-blind ("If I kept pushing my glasses up like you, I'd have to refocus every time": in other
words, she has to aim at pinpoints of sight), and it's a little silly de-
ciding where she should live without considering this. Clare looking for a taxi in New York, I later learn, is a plucky but nerve-rack-
ing spectacle.

Still she talks of bursting out of her rut and maybe she will. All
is possible once the nostrils flare. Since that winter, she has taken a
canal trip through Europe, which made living on a barge seem
briefly attractive, and even while writing this, I have received a
postcard from her out of Thailand, lamenting the poverty and the
panic in the air as the next domino girds itself. She has a great-step-
daughter in tow, a symbol of her complete rapprochement with the
Luces.* She hopes to make it to India to see Indira Gandhi ("Nehru
was the only man who ever made Harry jealous," says a friend) but
feels she may run out of gas. Energy is really worse to lose than
money *or* looks. (She didn't make it to India that time, but since
then has mysteriously turned up in Hong Kong. What is her game?)

But right now, we're in the middle of her rut. And it might be
worth taking another look at the fur that lines the rut to see why it
isn't altogether unendurable.

I've mentioned the drop-ins—people like Teller and Mortimer
Adler and Senator Fulbright, who as a freshman gave Congresswoman Luce her first hazing back in 1942. Not a bad little guest list
for one week, even allowing for the local tycoons and admirals who
flesh it out. In Arizona or Hawaii, one stumbles upon these extras,
the last of the Luce era, and I'm sure that if one had a portfolio, one
would have a famous time with them. They puzzle me as much as
their doubles did back in Connecticut in 1949. They seem as imme-
morial as statues in some colonnade of Stuffed Shirts that turns up
like family furniture wherever she goes. One of them has a liberal
wife whom they all regard as slightly pixilated, though she seems
conventional enough to me. (In sober fact, the Honolulu drop-ins
are perfectly nice people, who are just not up to Clare's verbal
workouts, which thus take on the aspect of shadow-boxing.)

As for the flora, Hawaii practically drips with it, a sea-bound
flower stall. And Clare's own house is a beauty. Picture if you will a
utopian ambassadorial residence that can accommodate every conceivable social occasion, situated on an island constantly fanned by

---

* It may seem strange to bring up invasion of privacy at this point. But somehow, perhaps primly, I don't feel the details of this belong in a book.

trade winds, under a sky fruity with birdsong. The question of why a woman who can live anywhere should choose to live here would not seem like a question at all to most people. Except for the wearisome jet trips she makes half a dozen times a year to Washington and New York, my wife couldn't think of any reason why Clare wouldn't want to live here. The house is elegant, roomy, and amazingly unshowy, considering the amount of stuff stashed here. There are some touches of pure Clare: the CBL monogram is still everywhere; and on a wall in the guest study, one finds hand-lettered in black on white in a small frame:

No good deed goes unpunished.
How beautiful it is to do nothing and rest afterward.
And above all, not too much zeal. (Talleyrand)

Moreover, the house is splendidly comfortable. Its eighteen- or twenty-foot ceilings don't overwhelm one because the furniture arrangements are as intimate as a cottage and attractive. Had she not been otherwise occupied, my wife (who knows about these things) believes that Clare might have been official decorator to the very rich. As, in a small way, she has been.

So her mild discontent does not call for food packages (book packages maybe). It entirely devolves on that life of the mind that she staked everything on so long ago: specifically the life of the mind in action, making things shake. In 1977, she has just served for some eight years on a presidential committee pithily called PFIAB—a mouthful of letters that defeats me, although "advisory board" seems reasonable—whose function it is to assess American global intelligence and see that we're getting the best. It must be a heady atmosphere to work in, because the members are much too important to be fobbed off with menial chores. They include such lights as Nelson Rockefeller and Big John Connolly and, in some capacity, that maid-of-all-work Henry Kissinger. Although PFIAB carries some liberals too, and seems more concerned with satellites than keyholes, it is probably too far right overall to survive the new Democratic Administration that is just about to land on us. Without it, Clare is left with such less specific but noisier forums as the unofficial Committee on the Current Danger—a group dedicated to the proposition that the Russians are always coming. Although the point of view suits Clare fine, it isn't, as I understand it, an *activity* like PFIAB, and it doesn't require the rapid intellectual judgments that spark Clare in the Hawaiian stillness.

We watch the Carter inauguration on Clare's set. It is too soon to get mad at Jimmy, and she observes that she can think of nothing so much as Huck Finn when she sees him. (Four years on in D.C., she will say she can't help it, she's *sorry* for Carter: such a splendid underdog.) On second thought, she remembers Joe Kennedy, who was another master of the inappropriate smile: Old Joe would light up at nothing at all, causing confusion on all sides. Joe leads to Jack, whom she liked inordinately. As a precocious young man, Jack had advised her against becoming a Catholic: it was tough enough for those born to it, but for her, it would be political suicide (so much for our first Catholic President). Later she returned the favor by advising Father Joe to discourage his son from running for Vice-President in 1956*—Stevenson was going to lose anyway, and Jack's vaunted Catholicism would get the blame. Clare and Jack undoubtedly liked and enjoyed each other, but they don't seem to have been very good at listening to each other. Jack ran for the nomination and lost it, the best possible outcome; Clare became a Catholic and committed political suicide—a sin against the Holy Ghost, according to a Kennedy.

Oddly enough, although there is talk aplenty about Madame Chiang, I can find no reference in my notes to those two other stalwarts of right-wing Asian policy, Mesdames Nhu and Chennault. Clare may not wish to be associated with a coven of dragon ladies, however much the public imagination likes the picture. Also, she takes détente with Red China more calmly than one might expect from Harry Luce's number one wife. Could it be that the China lobby was his baby more than hers all along? Thoughts for another time.

As the glittering past passes in review, Clare complains again about the lack of bright company in Hawaii. This is beginning to nag at something in my mind. It's true that there doesn't seem to be much talent around (though she hasn't tried the university), but Clare's collection of bores goes back a long way. As we rummage around, the past turns up its share of clods, along with its Kennedys and Churchills. Clare has, as noted earlier, always shown a strange taste for unprepossessing, misunderstood males, like Herbert Hoover, Cardinal Spellman, John Foster Dulles. Henry Luce, if you will. She told me with special admiration that Hoover could have all his teeth pulled in the morning and not mention it over dinner.

---

* As recorded in *Jack* by Herbert Parmet, published 1980 by Dial, New York.

Since something very like this happened to him politically, it's clear that his silence could be self-destructive and exasperating not just to himself but his party. (A clear account from Hoover of how FDR had refused to cooperate in New Deal-type measures during the interregnum of '32–33 would have removed at least some of the gloat from Democratic conventions. Indeed, Hoover revisionism is rapidly turning the Old Pudding into quite the reformer.) Nevertheless, Clare loved the sheer stoicism, as she did Nixon's over Watergate. "He's a fighter," she wrote of Tricky, in a much reviled letter to *Time* magazine.

Clare's friends from Column B I have found to be the hardest thing to explain about her. Insofar as her Hoovers and Spellmans are misunderstood, she buys a share of the misunderstanding, almost as if she welcomed the company. Nor for me the fens of psycho-history, but the flawed though gifted male is perhaps a not impossible analogue for a gifted woman: in each of the above cases, Clare seemed drawn toward a kind of sisterly alliance. Her Christmas cards and such to Dulles, while perfectly correct, are of a fondness and playfulness difficult to associate with that rhinocerine figure. But apparently Clare saw "a thin man trying to get out" (in Cyril Connolly's famous phrase) even in Dulles.

(Talking for the last time, I hope, of stoicism, Clare's literary agent of many years, Kay Brown, assures me that Clare did not just admire it in others, she practiced it faithfully herself. When her plays went wrong, she never blamed the critics or anyone else. She preferred to use her own chin. And she didn't even flinch when she learned that Max Gordon had inadvertently forgotten to protect the TV rights to *The Women* when he sold it to the movies. What's done is done, and she has never disputed the deal or even complained about it [sighed a little, maybe].

("She has been good for other business women," says Ms. Brown [and an agent would know], "because her word was solid gold and she never double-crossed a soul." So much for that part of her image.)

When we talked about Nixon, an interesting distinction arose, which may help to clear up the riddle of Clare's lumpy friends in general: the difference she allows between "like" and "respect." Did she respect Nixon? Yes. The most competent President she'd ever met. Like him? She hesitated, as if the question had never occurred to her. His private self, like her own, was quite unlike his weird public one, she explained. But *like* either one of them? Not especially, I gathered.

For most of us, I suppose, that would settle it: we would agree to respect the man from a safe distance. But a politician cannot always do this. And Clare's education in achievement really makes it possible for her to enjoy the company of someone purely out of respect, as one might enjoy a virtuoso musician with a rotten personality. Nixon's competence is enjoyable *in itself*. A lucid dissertation on geopolitics is worth any amount of charm. Even Kissinger, whom she at that time considered "sneaky," and whose embraces with Dobrynin reminded her of two prizefighters about to kill each other, was good value at dinner.

Just to prove that Clare is not alone in this chilly world, I later asked Mr. Kissinger himself what it was like working with Clare on their presidential committee. "She can cut right to the heart of a problem," rumbled the Doctor. "And cut the heart right out," said an interloper (we were not alone). "Yes," said HK, "she is not a warm lady."

Not with Kissinger she isn't. At the poker table with the men, warmth doesn't beat a low pair. In fact, to win the compliment (which seems sincere), she may feel she has to invite the insult. In a chauvinist polity, warm ladies finish last.

But long before she'd heard of politics, dull men were part of any girl's life, whether she was going places or not. Clare no doubt dated men she didn't much care for, and possibly married a man, Brokaw, she didn't much care for: none of this was unusual for the time. One treasured a man one could at least respect, a Baruch or Luce, while keeping open another track for pure friends, like Buffy Cobb or Donald Freeman at *Vanity Fair* or Letitia Baldrige, her flamboyant press secretary in Rome, and a hundred other warm, convivial souls. Of course, there were people she both liked and respected—Churchill, Eisenhower, sporadically Luce—but the two values remained quite distinct.

It helps here to remember the world Clare grew up in before the electric guitar had come to brighten our lives and when you still had to pump the Victrola every three minutes or so to hear a whole tune.

When Clare was young, and for quite a while longer (I remember the tail of the era), boredom was a fact of life, almost the air we breathed. One didn't expect to be entertained at church or school or even musicales; and as for the gaslit evenings at home, "Lord, they were dull," said my grandmother. Perhaps an aunt would drop in to sing "Abide with Me"; but outside of that, things were pretty slow.

It is small wonder that women forced to dwell like this finally took an ax to the saloons where all the fun was and gave us Prohibition. But that's another story. Young Clare's household seems to have been one of the jollier ones, but the general standards were still honored: character was more important than personality; humor, charm, etc., were all very well in their way, but they were not *values*; in fact, likability tended to indicate, if anything, weakness. Ideally, one had heroes, not "favorites," and even one's friends were to be judged on their wholesomeness, whether they were good influences or the other kind. (Just as there were two kinds of girls, there were two kinds of friends: the ones who were fun and the ones you brought home.)

All of these precepts bit deep into the serious-minded Clare: at any rate, she still honors heroes and she still admires character as such, even if the only manifest sign of it is the ownership of United Roller Skates, Inc. Her weakness for such people is not just a love of Power, of which she has sampled better stuff than this. I believe it is more like a vestige of the old-time American religion, whereby a solid businessman brought grace to one's parlor and boredom was not a factor. "Watch out, Harry, you'll drop the college," said Britt Hadden famously to Harry Luce, almost defining the beau ideal, the culmination of this stern dream. A man capable of carrying Yale was just the man to take you over the threshold. So if she finds Hawaii dull, I believe that a small part of her likes it that way.*

The paradox is that while Clare's success may seem like the last word in worldliness, it is rooted like the Great Fortunes in old moral precepts: patience, fortitude, hard work. God helps those who help themselves. The playful side of Clare cohabits strangely with the moralist, producing in recent years a species of jaunty sermon peculiarly her own: essays on the Good Man and the Good Society written with a straight face, like the funny teacher trying to bring the class to order. When Bishop Sheen asked her to be one of the lectors at his last Good Friday Mass, she accepted with all due gravity and humble pride; but when the bishop went into one of his lengthy spiels about "grant thy servants this" and "grant thy servants that," she found herself thinking involuntarily, "And while Thou art up, grant thy servant a double martini." The other Clares are never far away.

---

* I should add the other parts come leaping to life in Washington and New York, where she has invariably introduced me to bright people.

## MONKS AND GENERALS

The centerpiece of the Winter Palace, or Honolulu living room, is a glass table full of medals, worth, in sum, a bit more than a college degree. Anyway, they'll have to do. Clare still enjoys her honors gleefully (which is better and more civilized, in my view, than pretending you don't, crabbily) and the last few years have been especially rich with them, including a most gratifying bow from our stiff-waisted Congress itself in the form of its Distinguished Service Award, accompanied by a stack of letters from both sides of the aisle congratulating her warmly and fondly. She even relishes that torture chamber, the college auditorium, and the high point of her whole career may well have been her acceptance in 1979 of the Sylvanus Thayer award, West Point's highest honor, never before given to a woman. (Although she was not so dazzled by the occasion that she failed to notify me of the weight problems of the first women cadets: the Constitution guarantees equal calories, but not equal metabolism, she says. Life on the platform would be unendurable if one didn't keep one's eye out for things like that.)

The Thayer award was particularly sweet because it showed that the Army cared. For years Clare has carried a torch for it, as if she had been the one who'd gone to military school; but although she never met a general she didn't like, her greatest all-time hero gave her little good reason to love the Army. This is an unlikely fellow called Homer Lea, a turn-of-the-century figure who gave the military establishment quite a hard time of it and who had the kind of career she can most easily dream about. Lea was short and physically underendowed for a warrior, so he had to make do with guts and brains. In fact, he spent his best years beating his head against the brass, trying to prove a point, which was proved rather gaudily for him on December 7, 1941. It seems Lea had prophesied down to the smallest detail the Japanese strategy for World War II, long before anyone thought there would be a World War II. (Lea died in 1912, so of course he had to predict World War I as well in order to get to World War II, which was child's play for him.) And if all this did not precisely make him a great prophet—because the Japanese studied his work closely and did just what they were told—it did make him a notable strategist: also a hero unhonored in his time and vindicated later, Clare's type of guy. The author of *Europe in the Spring* has a soft spot for Cassandras.

Her love affair with the one career she couldn't swing may ac-

count for her amusement over the portly ladies of West Point. Anyway, it dates back at least to the forties, when she was looking for
something, anything solid to hang on to, and it slightly predates her
discovery of Peter's Rock. By chance, I got a glimpse of how her
two enthusiasms, martial and spiritual, have held up over the years
in a single fall day in Charleston, 1978.

"Did you find Jerry Ford in fine fettle?" somebody asked.
"He was in fettle," said Clare diplomatically. Ford is like a rel-
ative you have to visit now and then, with nothing much to report.
*You* know, he's still working at Prudential or Tool & Dye.

Clare and he had just attended a ceremony on the battleship
*Yorktown*, of which Harry had once written her, "I could not love
thee, dear, so much loved I not the Yorktown more." The Lovelace
line apparently brought down the house, compared with Jerry's
"We must have peace *through* strength," or whatever.

We pick Clare up at the Citadel in Charleston, where she has
been celebrating Mark Clark's 5th Army's annual reunion, a wistful
occasion as "the thin red line gets thinner every year" (CL). This is
her special army, and they have even resurrected her former WAC
aide-de-camp to escort her around. "If Italy was the soft under-
belly," she tells the aging heroes, "you should all have such under-
bellies now."

Military punctilio makes a nice background for her, the disci-
plined courtesy of the brass being warm but not cloying, scrupulously modulated, thus leaving her a little space. (A comparable
group of businessmen might gush too much, burying her in a syrup
of praise.) The Citadel compound is crisp and white, though a little
bit frayed, like the peacetime Army itself. One feels braced to be
there, walks out with shoulders straight, salutes a passing shavetail.
Shape up, my good man.

We are going from one Clare setting to another: from a military monastery to a Trappist one called Mepkin, which used to be
the Luces' southern retreat, the place where Harry spared the lives
of so many ducks, and Clare didn't. Here the welcome is very effu-
sive, in the manner of priests in old movies, whose "warmth" was
like a cast-iron shield, and it looks for an uneasy moment as if they
are buttering up the patron.

But Trappists are tricky. Being released from almost perpetual
silence by guests, the talk bubbles out gratefully like fizz from a
bottle. As this subsides, they turn out to be quite urbane and judi-

cious talkers and the abbot grills me especially closely on whether Flannery O'Connor might possibly be overrated (I say, no). They genuinely seem to love Clare, because she considers them her last family and I have never seen her more relaxed or less "public." At some point, an old fellow of ninety-three comes pottering up to greet her. "You're deaf and I'm blind," says Clare. "We're a fine pair." "The next time we'll meet in heaven," says the priest. "I'll remember you." "He's deaf but he still sings," mutters one of the Trappists, as it might be your wise-guy uncle.

If Trappists like to talk, they truly love to eat, and this is something else that guests license for them in good measure on rare occasions. To do both at once is very heaven, and we have the noisiest of lunches (homemade dove and quail stew) until Clare actually complains about the monkish decibels. One of the men is demonstrating at her request Trappist sign language, and it turns out that the symbol for President is a somewhat indecent one. "We had it first," says the monk innocently. Somebody points out that they could eat like this every day if only they had a doctor's permit. So one of the guests, who chances to be a gynecologist, suddenly finds herself besieged by three Trappist applicants for her services.

It is clear that these are no waxen Hare Krishnas living out a fad, but naturally exuberant men who love the things they've given up for God. Somehow they do not seem complicated enough for such a decision, but who knows? They might tell you that that's the whole point. We attend one of their masses, and in full assembly they seem trained fine from fasting and hard work, and their ceremony is sharp, like the early run of a play. Later they may be seen bicycling off in jeans to tend the 41,000 chickens, which are the monastery's meal tickets.

Undoubtedly Henry VIII's visitors would have closed the place anyway: a gorgeous 7,000-acre estate with forty ascetics rattling around in it. (Mepkin used to be even bigger when the Luces rattled around in it, but that would have been okay with Henry's visitors.) After her daughter's death, Clare could no longer bear to go there for pleasure, and this was an ingenious way of keeping it and letting it go at the same time. The expansionist abbot of Gethsemani, Kentucky, who was currently riding high on Thomas Merton's cassock tails and paperback sales, was only too happy to take it, and I dimly remember the Luces' ironic discussion of this back in 1949 while the deal was being completed. They were onto the abbot's game but did not think less of a priest for being a shrewd businessman. And what better way to retire the place that Ann Brokaw had loved more than any other in the world?

Clare immediately moved both her daughter's and her mother's remains to Mepkin, where they now share adjoining graves. And then, to everybody's surprise, it turned out sometime later that Presbyterian Harry had decided to join them, and he was buried in the middle, after a nervous ecumenical service. The cost-conscious abbot of the moment suggested a double tombstone with Clare's name on it too, cutting off, as she notes, all possibilities of future husbands, new religions, etc., although I did spot room for a modest postscript. So this is what she sees when she goes down there: her own tombstone and Harry's, with a shady tree sculpted above the names, and to either side her mother, Ann Clare, and her daughter, Ann Clare, in a grove of oak and cypress and Spanish moss, running down to the Cooper River. "She's taking it pretty well this year," says former Abbot Anthony. "She's usually very disturbed by this."

Monks & Generals: decorum, passion under wraps, ritual camaraderie. If a woman wants to be one of the boys, she has to choose her boys with care. With the Army, one might enjoy the respectful, housebroken whistle of a stray GI, but more than that would obviously be unmanageable. The officers' club is the only place for a woman, whether she likes it or not.

Clare's role in World War II and her swashbuckling foreign policy ever since must be considered in this light among others. Not for me to whitewash a cold warrior: a hard line hardens you, whether it's correct or not. But Clare's apparent militarism also has a Chocolate Soldier side: the Army in World War II, as laundered for Congresswoman Luce, was marvelous company. It was masculinity on its best behavior, power under restraint. Harry Luce could well have been a general himself: a dynamo with a stammer.

One pictures the generals of World War II falling in love with Clare in a body, like the whole student body of Oxford jumping into the river over Zuleika Dobson. Not literally, of course, but as she talks about them, there is a lingering echo of comradeship unmatched in her secular anecdotes. In fact, we did a whole tape about generals. The greatest natural soldier she ever met was Lucien Truscott II, who once gripped her knee in a tipsy vise ("Most great soldiers drink a lot") and asked her if she knew what the greatest thing in the world was. "Screamingly, I mean squirmingly," Clare said she couldn't imagine. And after a dramatic and paralyzing pause, Truscott said, "It's an American Division. You take my division. Is there anything you want done? You want somebody to deliver a baby? You want somebody to put on an opera? It doesn't matter what you want. Somebody in my division can do it and fight like hell too."

It is still rumored in the Truscott family that Luce and Lucien II had an affair, but it's no use asking because Clare never kisses and tells. Unlike her severe critic, Ms. Lawrenson (if only she would just *kiss* and tell), Clare would consider it dishonorable even when the bodies are cold. Such rumors kept us all going through a difficult war, and who knows how many generals' families still have similar stories to tell about Clare. She admits to landing under a table with Truscott during a raid, and she talks of him very fondly. "Imagine, a boy from Kansas being the conqueror of Rome," he said to her one night in the Colosseum. Gruff, nuggety, honest— Truscott was certainly her type. "But listen," says an old friend, "at our age you're delighted to hear about any old affair you're supposed to have had." Clare says only that she was too official to be anything more than flirted with.

Her great friendship with Eisenhower was the culmination of her infatuation with a Profession as such. Her first Ike story to me actually concerned his stinginess, or at least his mastery of the old soldier's game of scrounging. She bet some acquaintances that she could get something for nothing out of Ike, and after dinner one evening she asked him for a cigarette and casually reached for the whole pack, only to find the Great Compromiser tugging implacably at the other end.

However, she did get her second career out of him, in the form of the Roman ambassadorship and the Brazil fiasco—although not quite for nothing. *Time-Life* gave Ike fulsome support, to the disgust of its more right-wing subscribers and presumably advertisers. In return, Luce got John Foster Dulles as Secretary of State, and so on: these trade-offs, if that's what they were, are too complicated to trace to a single personal factor (Ike even switched to Harry's religion, Presbyterianism). Suffice it to say that, since World War II, Clare has thought more and more like a general herself.

Or perhaps a general's wife. In the WW II era, if you were one of the boys, you had to "enjoy being a girl," because there was "nothing like a dame." (These Oscar Hammerstein lines, which you could now only say in a dark room to trusted friends, were universally applauded in the forties and fifties.) This has been called the

Feminine Mystique, and the generals would not have liked Clare at all if she didn't exude it unstintingly. Since this mystique was simply a nationwide attempt to revive the style of her girlhood years anyway, a convulsion of nostalgia in a world of Auschwitz and Hiroshima, Clare took the feminine mystique in her stride. It was what she had been doing all along, and doing very well with (the feminine mystique propelled its best practitioners higher than anything since).

As a bridge figure between the courtesan and the career girl, Clare has sometimes seemed a funny kind of feminist, the women's movement finds her a difficult patron saint. She wanted to do all the things that men did, but if she didn't need a man under the bed, she needed one behind the throne. After all, she didn't have a movement in back of her. I've mentioned the grouching that I still hear about the specially built latrines (called "The Women") that announced her arrivals in Italy, but I imagine the amusement and jock-strap jollity were greater. These were the terms on which she swashbuckled; the first woman to do certain things cannot completely do them, because she has to do them *as a woman*, a special mode. So now as an honorary U.S. general her role remains essentially womanly: to echo the Pentagon somewhat uncritically and to scold its enemies fiercely. Her singular contribution, as always, is to phrase their needs more pithily than the powerful stammering males can.

Pithiness wounds, of course, but Clare's tongue is absolutely the only violent thing about her. Otherwise, her relationship with warriors is as ritualistic as her relationship with monks. She doesn't go to war, and I was about to say she doesn't go to church either (not excessively, anyway, so long as they play guitars there). What she does in each case is exchange courtesies: a toast, a blessing, a few bright words of endorsement and affection. Symbols are tremendously important to her, whether a tombstone or her large collection of medals. She likes the *idea* of monks, and the idea of strong chivalrous men defending our borders. Both groups live for a dream outside themselves, sacrificing vanity and self-interest, at somebody else's command. After what she has been and seen, after the poisoned jungles of *The Women* and the gouging of Washington, unselfishness in *any* cause can seem reassuring.

On this drowsy day at Mepkin, it feels as if the peace she sought so desperately when she became a Catholic has been found for now at least: since her turbulent entry in 1946, she has settled into a calm float. The Church, she says, steadied her then, so that for the first time she didn't feel like a lost child. Before that, "I felt I'd been blown into things, some very nice, but always blown. . . . The Church was like being acquired by a noble family."

The family was probably even more important than the ideas, though she wrestled manfully with these, wading through "miasmas of doubt." But one wouldn't want to lose a noble family over some footling miasma. If the Church was true, it was the only place to be. Other churches might save you as well, but not half so agreeably. She had never had a warmer reception anywhere, despite a slight chill from certain Irish elements who didn't believe that you could be a Republican and a Catholic at the same time. Apart from that, there was in those days a bland "goodness" among middling-to-rich Catholics worthy of a Dickens last chapter. As a pleasant footnote she also lost a secretary, an anti-papist from South Carolina who wouldn't even answer the Catholic mail, and gained instead Dorothy Farmer, the friend she "loves the most."

All in all, a good deal. The hot religious honeymoon cooled into "dailiness" a good while ago, but the Church distrusts enthusiasm anyway. John Courtney Murray, the Luces' Richelieu, "thought I trusted too much in the goodness of God, and should be more formally a Catholic," which is standard wet-blanket therapy. In fact, she has followed his advice about halfway. During the Kiss of Peace at the Trappist mass, where you touch and say "May the peace of Christ be with you," she kissed her neighbor (me) and said, "Hi."

As our day in Charleston indicates, she keeps in close touch with both families, all the fathers and brothers of the Sword and the Cross. They synthesize briefly that afternoon as she tells the abbot about her recent writings calling for a strong foreign policy. The abbot nods thoughtfully; it seems like good sense to him. But he appears as detached about it as a general talking theology. He doesn't strictly need a foreign policy for himself and his community. Whatever happens to the world, a Trappist has very little to lose. He is like someone to whom the war has already happened. So he is a fallback if her other family fails her. If all the terrible things that she fears come to pass and we appease our way into cataclysm, the holy men will still be practicing there, love and order as before, a family among the ruins.

\*   \*   \*

I have seen Clare a number of times since then, finding each time that whatever detachment I came in with had diminished by that much more. After a while it began to seem silly whipping out a notebook whenever a friend opened her mouth, or writing up solemn accounts of lunches and dinners. Murray Kempton says that if a criminal trial lasts longer than a year, the jury will vote to acquit, regardless of the evidence. So it goes with this kind of work. One's usefulness as an observer fades from overexposure.

So just like that I put away my notebook and decide to quit for now. The stories keep tumbling in over the transom about the other Clare who acts sassy or high-handed at parties, etc., but I'm resigned to the prospect of never meeting her. She is clearly not for me.

The last time I saw my version was on a day in December 1980. Bill Buckley's *National Review* is throwing itself a Twenty-fifth Anniversary bash at which Clare is to speak. So we have lunch together and talk, among other things, about speaking—the tricks of timing that make a joke better than it is, the automatic laugh lines that people *have* to respond to, as they respond to an anthem, and which loosen them up for the good stuff. I contend that these and other devices ruin one for straight writing, and she doesn't disagree. She is now primarily a speechwriter anyway, and when I read her transcripts I simply turn on her voice and listen.

It is one of our "how to" talks from way back. In a gray business suit, with her hair fluffy and unworked over and her daytime glasses on, she could be a bright executive on the way up. Ronald Reagan is about to mount the throne, and while she doesn't crow over it in the least—her only comment on the New Right ascendancy concerns Margaret Thatcher: "Why do middle-class English women always feel they have to wear huge bows on their bosoms?"—it does open up Washington again: maybe even a jog on her old intelligence advisory committee ("Nothing famous. I've had quite enough of that"). On the strength of her lunchtime appearance, I would hire her on the spot.

Afterwards, we taxi over to Elizabeth Arden for work on the evening Clare. And when I see her next at Buckley's, she is gussied up beyond recognition in a pink gown (my wife *thinks* it was an orange and pink caftan, whatever that means) and spanking beauty-parlor hairdo. Her eyes look pale and slightly out of focus in contact lenses. She is regal indeed, but the young executive is nowhere to be seen. For the first time that day, you might even guess close to her age.

Her speech is about excellence, as embodied for tonight in Bill
Buckley and throughout history by people who have dared to stand
above the herd, the plebs, the common man. "Tacky, *tacky,*" I hear a
lonesome liberal mutter. But at least Clare is not talking about some
sort of class distinction. Excellence is there for anyone willing to
heft it and carry it, like Yale, on his back. Greatness is an act of will.

I think of my father's comparison of Clare to a Roman matron.
Agrippina on a rostrum in the forum. (All the famous Roman
women were villains. It was the price back then, too.) The *virtus*, the
*pietas*, the stoic virtues are all there, shining fiercely in this seventy-
seven-year-old lady: love them or leave them, but they are not
tacky.

The conservatives in the audience, who are presumably not the
titans Clare has been describing, applaud the speech tepidly: perhaps they find it a little old-fashioned. To me it harks back not just
to Ayn Rand but to Clare's old hero Bernard Shaw and his *Man and
Superman.* Shaw was, of course, a bouncy Fabian Socialist, but he
was also a Nietzschean *Obermenscher,* a darker matter, and in this
Clare was a Shavian woman. It is no accident that she played Candida in her one grown-up tilt with the stage in the forties: she could
have played—did in fact play—several bits and pieces of Shaw's
heroines in real life, from Eliza Doolittle to Cleopatra and more. But
Candida is an especially interesting example. If you recall, the lady
in question was obliged to choose between a stuffy but decent husband and a somewhat bratty young poet. This was not precisely the
lineup at Ridgefield in 1949, and it certainly wasn't the story, but
the superficialities were sufficiently in order for her to play her finest Candida of all that Summer.

Clare also shared Shaw's dynamist philosophy, if not his politics, to the hilt, although he makes a strange bedfellow for the
American Dream. Shaw wanted nothing less than a superior race to
replace our own rather messy one, and he talked of how he hoped
someday to pass this torch from his own exhausted hand to a new
generation. Tonight Clare was handing out her own torch as usual:
but, as with Shaw himself, there didn't seem to be too many takers.
Unlike Shaw (perhaps? perhaps not), I don't think she expected
any.

On the way home, it occurs to me for the first time—I'd have
been faster with an English person—that Clare's upper-class accent
may have been what maddened the hatchet-women at *Vanity Fair*
and elsewhere the most. It is easy to call it fake, because upper-
class accents are all fake: learned from the memory of some folk

speech. But Clare's is real enough, and all the more maddening for that in the American thirties.

"It's a pity you've finished your book" says Clare on the phone today, making one of her rare references to this thing here.

Little does she know. Thrusting my arm into mothballs, I retrieve the notebook. Clare, it seems, wants to report an attack of envy. After so many years on the receiving end, it is a novel sensation. "Which is it, jealousy or envy?" she wonders. After kicking this around, we agree on envy as the more abstract and potentially deadly of the two. "Because I don't want to *be* her. I would just like to have had that kind of chance."

The subject was Sandra O'Connor, the first woman appointed to the Supreme Court, and no doubt that magic word "first" was part of the temptation. But what Clare talked about mostly was the simple opportunity to enter law school and all the other schools which were closed to her and which lead to the real prizes: not the shiny medals and the honorary degrees, but the real stuff.

"I wouldn't want the job now. Seventy-eight has insinuated itself, sneaked up on me in the most contemptible way." No, this is her teen-age self still envying the one that got away: a court instead of courtiers, jurisdiction as opposed to laying down the law. As it is, she has had to settle more recently for being sent by President Reagan to General Marcos' inauguration in the Philippines—the one kind of thing a girl *could* learn in school in those days, and which Clare learned the hell out of. "If you're ever offered a flight on Air Force I," she adds, "feel honored, and don't take it." I make a note of this.

Envy seems to have cheered her up, breaking out a new bag of dreams. "When I was young," she freewheels, "a really successful man had to own a railroad and have an opera star for a mistress. Now what? Own a newspaper? have a model for a mistress? or is that changing?"

It's all a great farce, anyway. The bubbles that come and go. Who remembers the men with the railroads now and who cares? We drift into family talk, which at least has some substance to it.

Still. A seat on the Supreme Court would have been really something.

# Epilogue: Big Pictures and Little Ones

However many books one writes, or tries to, one enters each one, like the New Year, as a child and leaves as an old man. This chapter began as an introduction and kept getting pushed farther and farther back. I finally decided not to let it fall off the end, because it represents my thoughts as I started out, before plunging into the undergrowth of memory and detail. It is the proposition I set out to prove, or disprove, or both, as I scribbled away the first days in Hawaii, 1977, and the first few weeks back on the mainland. Note how abstract and quasi-Toynbeean I still was about careers and legends. I couldn't be that way now.

In the 1920s, the United States was subject to random explosions of energy, like uncoordinated fireworks. The crazy genetic drive that had overwhelmed a continent in the last century was still at large, but looking for something to do, like fans after a game. If the drive found something useful, like flying the Atlantic, so much the better. Otherwise, it sat on flagpoles or danced for days or simply drank its brains out, banging its head against the walls it had erected itself in its fever of construction.

Clare Boothe Luce looked like one of these explosions, a sort of Charles Lindbergh of women's rights and possibilities. Editor, playwright, congresswoman, ambassador (the twenties did not entirely take place in the twenties), the trophies themselves were impressive enough, in a Guinness Book of World Records sort of way. But what was new about Clare, aside from her improbable beauty, was the sense of sky's-the-limit potency, the feeling that it could have been any *other* four trophies, or eight; that this woman would take on anything and master it with sheer gusto. It was the American Woman as Dynamo, a Jules Verne–like phenomenon and an answer to the Great Men of the previous era who were famous just for being successful. The "success story" that flourished when Clare was a girl didn't really care whether you cornered steel or Grape-Nuts: it simply celebrated your energy and willpower. And your virility. So Clare as Success Woman was admired just for doing things, never mind what things. It was her essence they wanted: the details, as with George Washington Carver, were incidental.

Naturally, Clare became, like Lindbergh, larger than life: a vulnerable condition in a peeping Tom society. In Lindbergh's case, the distance between the man and his image was almost too painful to watch when he went public in the thirties–forties—although once he remembered to shut up and look wise, the image reformed itself in a smaller way of business. But with Clare the image and the person were thought to be one. She always seemed to be "on," always herself, still larger than life, for better or worse, like a Disneyland balloon. She is one of the few famous people I can think of who is practically never called complicated. ("Complicated" simply means inconsistent in most cases. See Nixon's foreign policy.)* Devious, yes—but even people who call her that feel that they're onto her game. Being transparent is part of her persona. Her very name, clear and lucid, seems to abet this.

Her public persona, that is, which stands guard over the private one, intercepting callers and handling all appearances. Close friends know that she is one of the few celebrities who actually deserves to be called "complicated" as opposed to just confused or emotionally unstable. Private Clare is startlingly different from Public Clare—and Private Clare is several people too.

However, one must start and end with the lady who opens the

---

* I leave this in for its musty, dated quality, like that of a Bob Hope political joke.

door: a grande dame by now, of slightly old-fashioned high-comedy theatricality, harking to a time when great ladies *were* great ladies. She enjoys the role so thoroughly that everyone else enjoys it too. It is combined with a great naturalness, as if this was the way she was meant to be from the very first. Old fights are forgotten, by all but the incurably mean-spirited (a sturdy contingent). She has, on this particular day, just sent a message of commiseration to Barbara Walters, who has been getting some flak over her bloated salary at ABC. "I know just how she feels," says our pioneer career woman, like a veteran comforting the latest wounded.

"Remarkable" is the word one uses on the way out, as of a great force of nature: to see someone come through like this, in such high style and spirits, is heartening, whoever you are. A great old age is her least controversial achievement, and it somehow validates the others. Enduring, staying on her feet to the end, seems to be part of her proposition, her wager with Fate.

The image was not always so benign, or perhaps it didn't look so good on a younger woman. Because although she was often on the most-admired lists (in the Land of Amnesia, people have trouble naming ten of anything) she was also on the other one that never got published: the most hated; and she knew it. The public need to hate had sorted her out early, for its own good reasons. Clare was the right myth at the right time: so she played a part in social history not entirely of her choosing and became this "character" that everyone knew about, even though they knew nothing about her. How did this come to pass?

Norman Mailer, the tour guide to celebrity, has described a metaphysical presence which accompanies him everywhere, and which consists half of what he pretends to be and half of what the others expect him to be. Clare's equivalent comes in different proportions. Nobody needs a Mailer; he is free to invent himself. Clare *had* to be invented. The first pure Success Woman had to be a bit of a bitch.

As with other scientific phenomena, there is less freedom in this area than meets the eye. Certain types recur in all generations. In the economy of celebrity, every denizen works like an ant to perform some socially useful task: to be outrageous, to be predictable, to edify us or to Pay The Price. Fame is not free. When a Truman Capote pillories his Café Society friends in print, he is only exacting their Entertainment Duty. If they want to be onstage, at those prices, they have to *do* something. And if they don't like it—

well, their parts are constantly up for audition by those who do, by Eve Harringtons* primping in the next room.

Clare Luce's best analogy remains the theater, where the question resolves itself quickly into how many women's parts were available in the great national play. Whatever there were, Clare seemed at times to be trying out for all of them, including the ones where you dress as a boy—but this in itself is a part: the woman who wants everything. So alongside Clare the versatile, we get Clare the opportunist, playing stage mother to her own career and getting the part somehow, even if she has to lock a rival in the bathroom and marry the producer.

The role played sensationally well for years, proving how much we needed it. When, on my return from Hawaii, I put a note in *The New York Times*, requesting Clare Luce memorabilia, I was startled by the number of letters I got from older people who didn't even know her, commanding me to destroy the bitch, and passing on stale tales of her pushiness and arrogance (the other half told of equally extreme kindness). In my dreams I can still hear the Pope telling her again and again, "But, madam, I too am a Catholic"; others have her ordering limousines to take her across the street or telling important people to mind her sables for her, or even in one case wearing too much makeup, which is worth noting for its vintage spuriousness: heavy makeup would have caved in her famous skin long before her current seventy-eight. But "that kind of woman" always wears too much makeup.

In short, just as Dorothy Parker can't lose an anecdote, Clare Luce can't win one with this gang. In the perfect Clare story, this highly intelligent woman invariably winds up sticking her painted foot in it, or getting her comeuppance from some Dorothy Parker or other; the shrewdness that got her to the top, and enabled her to write a skillful anatomy of the top called *Stuffed Shirts* while still on the way up, apparently deserts her at the simplest social encounter, according to my correspondents.† In a movie, she would be the other woman, the snob, the glittering fool, who invariably loses the man. Only in real life could such a one flourish.

---

* For those pure souls who don't attend movies, Eve Harrington (Ann Baxter) is an aspiring actress who climbs to the top of her trade over the carcass of her "idol" (Bette Davis) in *All About Eve*.

† Clare reminds me that there is another school of anecdotes in which *she* plays Parker, in order to put down someone else the teller doesn't like. These I find more believable. But Clare says they're mostly air bubbles like the rest.

Indeed, the Clare stereotype turns up so often in movies and plays of the period (played by various versions of Eve Arden) that it hardly even needed Clare: the new career woman, using her brains and sex competitively, had the nation boggled, and the first response had to be caricature. She had to fail in fiction, because she failed so seldom in fact. Characteristically, Clare saw this quicker than anybody and she wrote (in *The Women*) easily the most successful caricature of her own "type" getting its lumps. But this didn't help a bit. *The Women* was simply taken to be a sort of group picture of Clare. In fact, it could be argued that Clare the monster didn't really get off the ground until she'd written the part and circulated it.

Since I have never seen a trace of this horror film persona in our meetings, I have had to guess how much she made it up herself, and how much of it is a confabulation of wish-think, a public demand for that kind of character. Relaxing between performances, she gives (like Muhammad Ali) no hint even of what *kind* of act she does—so long as you are alone with her, and no dinner table is in sight. In fact, the *last* act I would have expected from Clare is the one she's famous for. Alone, she does not begin to qualify for her own legend, her own anecdotes.

Still, all that hissing and applauding must be about *something*, even if I can't see it from my stagehand's perch. The audience wants a certain kind of show, and the performer wants to give a certain kind of show, but there are limits to how far apart they can be. Clare cannot be based entirely on a misunderstanding: she must want to be *something like* the woman she seems. But one man's "gutsy" is another man's "ruthless," and there is often this slight lack of sync between the performer and what appears on the screen.

I shall try not to make this a feminist tract, because Being a Success affects so few people of either sex that its problems are rather special—though no doubt some damn fool would call it a macrocosm. Macro or micro, it seems likely that, from prehistory through most of Clare's lifetime, a woman has had less control over the performing contract, less say in her image-building, than a man, if only because of those fewer parts. Like a member of the Royal Family who can only be a Bad Thing or a Good Thing, an Edward or a George, a woman must choose from a small supply of masks. We can always use a Florence Nightingale or two, and an old sage, and a great fool—and of course, an ever-fresh chorus of sluts. But the one absolute necessity is the heartless schemer, the cold climber, who takes different shapes in different periods depending on the terrain. In the 1920s, her type was still a fortune or title hunter, in the thirties she was more streamlined and managerial, a mistress of the boardroom: but in both cases, she still depended on men, their care and manipulation.

In the twenties, Clare married her pointless millionaire George Brokaw; and in the thirties, with her plans for a new picture magazine as wedge, she married purposeful, upthrusting Harry Luce. If she had done nothing else, and had kept her trap shut forever, she would have had the role right there. She had acted out not one but two of our favorite dreams. And she proceeded to do so many variations on them, like the great Dream Factory itself: Clare goes to Broadway, Clare goes to war, to Washington, to Rome. It was a splendid series, family entertainment for the millions, but it had to build up its underworld of deflating gags. Clare takes a bow that isn't called for, fires a cannon that she's not supposed to, calls Roosevelt a dying man at the worst possible moment, lectures the Pope, and gets poisoned by her own ceiling. The script *demands* that the climbing woman fall on her prat (did you ever hear a nice story about Wallis Simpson?), and the gossip industry does the rest.

As I say, all this is not based on nothing: the superhuman drive and self-belief that makes a career like hers possible can overflow into arrogance and self-satisfaction. I have even seen the delightful Lauren Bacall terrorizing Bloomingdale's. And Clare did have one besetting weakness—a lifelong craving to be thought clever—that is guaranteed to undo one occasionally. But it's my belief that *any* woman who had had that career would have had that reputation, or bits of it.

For instance, a number of the hearsay letters I got about Clare were from old *Time* magazine hands who seem corporately still to resent being upstaged by the boss's wife. Although Harry Luce celebrated their union by taking away Clare's picture magazine, and although *Time* usually went out of its way not to mention her, she was widely felt, as the scheming woman must be, to cast an invisible spell over Luce and his empire: particularly so by those furthest from the action. (Those on top seem inclined to like her.)

Clare had good reason to feel herself at some sort of war with the institution, if only for Harry's attention, and she called his underlings "Harry's little boys" often enough to unleash an army of professional gossips bent on vengeance. Whether she upstaged them first or they her, it's clear she made no special effort to mollify them. A Queen's got to do what she's got to do.

Then again, women who become famous in America, outside of the arts or good works, are commonly taken to be slightly comic figures. Think of Eleanor Roosevelt, Ma Perkins, Betty Friedan; or from earlier times, Susan B. Anthony (yes), Amelia Bloomer, Carry Nation—the latter reminding one of the way victims seem driven to confirm our prejudices about them. If women are supposed to be silly, they will find a way to do it, and Clare has not altogether escaped this curse. In a world where women are either saints or giddy fools, she has been alternately mistaken for both. And there is one more quaint invariable; every woman I can think of connected in a big way with publishing, whether Fleur Cowles or Kay Graham or Dorothy Schiff, has given birth to the same whisper: "Is it true she's a bitch?"*

In the period when Clare was growing up, women still had something called "a reputation" in whose shadow they lived completely. And of these the sharpest and most hatchet-faced was a reputation for ambition. If you had one of these, everything you did was poisoned, every act of kindness and gesture of friendship was tainted. Talk stopped on the veranda as you approached. Although there were mouth-watering fortunes to be made in America, no woman could show the slightest interest in one without becoming a bitch *and* a comic figure. Once you were observed to hustle, or even suspected of it, the game was up. Certain people would despise you forever, whatever you did: no earthly success would win the stone heart of Newport. You just learned to live with it. Clare keeps a file of letters called "Dear Clare, you bitch" to neutralize any flattery she now gets. I had never appreciated the tiara of thorns she had bought into until I saw this.

Clare's mother, as we have seen, taught Clare to think of ambition as the great American virtue, regardless of sex, and the daughter still can't see anything wrong with it. By now she has more company, and the myth of the Climbing Woman has receded in our dream life, but this was no help then. At that time it was Clare against the world, or so it must have felt. The Risen Woman

---

* Not quite an invariable, but more than a tendency, is a general suspicion of strong wives as such. I have, since writing this, heard countless people denounce Rosalyn Carter as a ruthless manipulator without offering one piece of evidence. Give us Bess Truman every time.

was even worse than the Fallen Woman. How did she get her money? Why did she marry Brokaw? Who did she sleep with, where did she come from, did she have voice lessons?

A lifetime of this can toughen your skin, and a thick skin can lead to mistakes. When Clare said something brutal about a public figure, it was tame compared with what she was used to getting herself, in her incredible private mail. Minorities may learn obsequiousness or magnanimity, but sportsmanship is harder; after you've been kicked around, you're just not in the mood for it. Having sampled a whiff of the bile she evokes, I'm surprised she hasn't played rougher.

Calling Clare a minority may seem odd, yet a self-made woman is surely the ultimate minority. And it made her a fighter, and respecter of fighters. It is no accident that many of her fans share this old-fashioned American virtue almost indiscriminately.* It was inevitable that when she defended Richard Nixon, it would be on the grounds that he, too, was a fighter—never mind for what or whom. For a generation that hasn't had to fight for anything, the praise lacked force—especially since Mr. Nixon seemed more like a punching bag. But "taking it" is very much part of fighting.

"I will lay me down for to bleed a while / then I'll rise up and fight again," she had quoted when she lost the senatorial nomination at the 1950 Connecticut Republican Convention, and Nixon quoted this back to her when he resigned ("he botched the quote" she admits). But bleeding well is almost the most important thing.

What rare mix of phantoms and real dangers Nixon fought has been analyzed at gloomy length elsewhere. But those were no phantoms Clare was up against. Making one's way into society from nowhere, and then carrying the scars over to Manhattan, journalism, Broadway, Luce, and Washington gave a woman real fights enough for several lifetimes. Clare's career is a guidebook to what a woman without inherited means thought she had to do to get ahead in this American century. And there's not a lot of evidence that says she was wrong. If she seemed at times pushy and calculating, the chances are we wouldn't be talking about her at all if she hadn't been. Alice Longworth and Eleanor Roosevelt could embroider received positions; Clare Luce hammered hers out of nothing. And even if those tough qualities had been better hidden, we'd have sus-

---

* Yet more recently Clare called in to say, "You know I'm supposed to get mad at those Iranian students on TV, but I'm only bored." Still the old fight songs must be sung occasionally.

pected them anyway from the results, and perhaps called her a hypocrite to boot. That the candor kid assuredly is not. She's too much a pushover for a clever phrase. And as an old journalist she appreciates a writer's need for a story. In the talks we've already had about this book, she has been amazingly open about herself, and only less so in cases where other people might be hurt. If you can get your own way without duplicity, you'd be a bumbling amateur to use it.

The other letters I received, which testified to private kindness, are as ardent as the nasty ones, and a lot more circumstantial. She does not want these talked about—it would spoil the whole point. But in fairness they should at least be mentioned. I wouldn't venture an analysis of charity, a virtue so basic that any account of it sounds glib, but the glib questions must at least be asked. Is generosity simply the other side of ambition, like a prizefighter getting the crowd on his side by buying drinks? Is kindness one more aspect of the career, or a spy from the other side? Is it conscience money or the real thing? I can only repeat that Clare's is Top Secret.* It is also impulsive—her imagination is easily stirred—but faithful in the follow-up. If she were to put someone through school, say, it would be all the way through and beyond.

Then, once again, there's Clare's politics. In late years, these have swarmed over her image to the exclusion of everything else. And since they are vociferously right-wing (in foreign policy at least), they divide the public on rather simple-minded grounds and make her somewhat too easy to judge. Neither her friends nor her foes seem to know much about her, except that they feel very strongly about it.

In this, she resembles her opposite number, Eleanor Roosevelt. In Eleanor's case, the liberals assumed she was reasonably smart, because liberal means smart; the Right assumed she was a well-meaning ass, because that's what liberal means over there. Thus this rather modestly endowed woman came in two versions so wildly different that no one cranium could house them both. Our right-left preconceptions are so strong that actual evidence can be disregarded. (In the words of Chico Marx, "Who are you going to believe—me or your own eyes?")

And so it goes counterclockwise with Clare: a sage to the

---

* Observe the impossible situation. Does one blow the secret, or leave a gaping hole in her character? I do a bit of both.

Right, a special pleader for her own wealth to the Left. And also, like Eleanor, the whole image further skewed by preconceptions about women. A male Eleanor Roosevelt would be unimaginable, though we've probably had several. Clare's particular loss was the half of the populace more likely to write books about her. Until recently her knee-jerk detractors were somewhat more articulate than her allies, so her own tongue had to do all the work. A woman the least conscious of image would surely have thought of this. So we may take her choice to turn right as quite sincere. It has cost her image plenty among the image-makers.

Since Clare and Eleanor believed completely in what they were doing, there is no need to go on a psychic fishing trip to explain their positions. Yet with both, one senses a willingness to make distant enemies (perhaps because it seemed inevitable) for the sake of close friends. The people who love you will love you very much indeed, if you're a stand-up partisan. The sense of a shared cause quickens life and fills it. And enemies validate this. Those of us who took part in peace marches remember how the pleasure gradually separated itself from the subject matter until we could have been marching for anything; and how one felt that something was missing if no hecklers showed up. One could easily make a way of life out of this.

"Man does not live by politics alone" wrote Christopher Dawson. I have always found the political reading of personality to be the most superficial; or alternately, that people who *can* be so read are the most superficial. One doesn't think any less of an Iowa farmer or a Texas oil man for not being a liberal Democrat. His politics reflect his interests, unless he's a kibitzer: a sage or a crank. Either way, they're probably the least interesting thing about him. And so I feel about Clare. Her politics make sense for her. Yet I also have a nagging conviction which may seem to contradict other things I've said, that they don't run very deep except as self-expression. At any rate, the fact that I don't particularly agree with them makes less difference to her than to almost anybody I know on that side.

She would always have been pugnacious, but it could have gone in other directions if her life had been different. If FDR had only paid attention in 1933, if she had stuck with playwriting . . . Still, it would be strange if Clare did not love a system which had made her possible; which had enabled a nobody to reach the top without just sleeping her way up. (Even the New Left treated its women less well than capitalism treated Clare.) A career like hers is seldom generated by a collectivist, and the American pantheon would be an empty place if we threw out all the individualists.

The career itself is what interests me, and the superhuman drive and self-determination that made it possible. Although, as I say, the American cult of success was at its goofiest in the 1900s, and the self-made man was king, it was for men only: a stag party. Women were supposed to do it some other way. Clare and Harry Luce must have both read reams about the men of iron who built this country and their own fortunes as if these were one and the same thing, and it was natural for Harry to emulate them. For Clare it was more complicated: the drive was constantly tempered and even derailed by the female condition. Her career only looks single-minded from a distance. Up close it is spasmodic, herky-jerky, unplanned—a series of disconnected challenges met or unmet. Success Woman never knew what, if anything, she was going to do next, but was simply, as she says, "blown about." Playing the wind, tacking, trimming, but always herself: this *was* the gift to which the other gifts were harnessed.

"What do you suppose my life means?" to get back to her question. "Do you suppose it means anything?" What does any adventure mean? It means something if you can get a story out of it—Jason and the Golden Fleece, Luce and the American Dream. Ironically, she has rather lost her taste for the women's movement and its antics (though she's an old friend of ERA), because the serious answer to her question has to lie in that direction. I know women who have been inspired to try things by the very idea of Clare, and there must be hundreds more who mightn't have attempted careers at all if it hadn't been for this patron saint of female success. If at times Clare's religion has been the most popular one in America, herself, she has always been equally true to the message that billowed from Mrs. Belmont's deck chair so many years ago.

Privately her life has had at least one satisfactory other meaning: she has woven a tapestry of friendship that only death itself can unravel. Each of her friendships is one of a kind, a small artwork: together they form a picture, a jigsaw of a life. One way this worked was the shared anecdote. If you and Clare ever did something together (whether dining in the Via Veneto, or being trapped in an elevator), she lived the experience so fully at the time and recalled it so inventively later that it was incorporated into the friendship. It assigned you your particular shape and color, so that when she talked of *other* friends, you knew who they were even if you'd only met them in her stories.

Other people, other pictures. My own will seem unrecognizable to some, but it is as faithful as I can make it.

Much to-do has been made lately about friendship between men, which is really just a chapter in the history of Anglo-Saxon embarrassment ("how do I tell him I love him?"), and not some basic new discovery. The real unknown territory is friendship between men and women. Platonic sounds wishy-washy, as if the parties were not up to anything stronger. Mother / son, brother / sister, etc., suggests that all experience is contained in the family condition. Clare's friendship, as I experienced it, was none of the above, not even aunt / nephew (we never drank sherry).

Many people assume that this leaves nothing but sexual, but they're wrong. Clare's friendship was more like that between members of the same sex in terms of ease and taking each other for granted, but with the pleasures of otherness added. But that's all the analysis it's going to get here. Just as the first person to say "Aren't we having a good time?" spoils the party, so the first friend to mention friendship breaks the spell like an alarm clock. But if I appear personally in this book a touch more than anyone remembers asking for, it's because Clare has to be seen through actual eyes. She belongs in scenes, constantly interacting with others, improvising, creating.

A last word.

"Do not defend me" is almost her heraldic motto, and I'll do my best not to. She is too widely admired—and not just by the simple peasantry and the oafish tycoonery, but by some of the brightest people I know—to need that. There is a good legend every bit as robust as the bad one. Nevertheless, I can't quite take my eye off the irreconcilables, if only because I might have been one myself if I hadn't met her first. The good legend needs no help from me, though I'll give it a poke from time to time.

Would I forgive something in Clare that I wouldn't in a man? It's a non-question because a man wouldn't have had to do the same things in quite the same way. It was a woman's career, one of a kind, to be judged or not judged as such. But if it wasn't a non-question, I'd be inclined to say yes; I would forgive it: because she was the first, cutting her way through a man's world that most women were scared even to enter, and making clearings for others in the future. Whatever one feels about the results, it was a colossal undertaking, and Clare's Bowie knife, her tongue and her wits, belong in whatever Hall of Fame is appropriate. And unlike most other pioneers I can think of, she has been almost unfailingly entertaining about it.

I would be surprised if a man finding his way in a world of Amazons would be half so good-humored and well balanced about it as Clare Boothe Luce.

# Index

## ABOUT THE AUTHOR

Twice nominated for a National Book Award in Fiction, Wilfrid Sheed is not only a successful novelist, but a frequent reviewer and essayist whose pieces appear in such magazines as *The New York Review of Books*, the *New York Times Book Review*, *Esquire*, and *The New Yorker*. He lives in Sag Harbor, Long Island.